Their Lives Reflected

Their Lives Reflected

A Treasury of Life Stories Captured Through The Legacy Project

Arielle S. Galinsky

First Edition
2020

Printed in the United States of America.

ISBN-13: 9798590230945

*In memory of my Papa Hilly & Papa Dave,
my rock stars.*

Table of Contents

Preface

It all started with regret.

Although difficult to admit, it is the truth. And I feel compelled to share the reality of how The Legacy Project, and later this book, came to fruition.

Regret.

As a little girl, I looked up to my grandfathers like they were rock stars.

Papa Hilly was the adventurous type, always eager and willing to take me to wherever my heart desired (or wherever my mother would *allow* him to take me). Whether it was watching trapeze artists at the circus, gazing at small residential planes taking off at Norwood Airport, or engaging in an intense round of bumper boating at the local mini-golf venue, it was always a grand time.

PREFACE

He was a wholehearted lover of the New England Patriots and peanut M&Ms, as well as a chess fanatic. He even taught me how to play the game at a young age—a skill I would often boast as a little girl. I remember my grandfather's sense of humor, always making others smile with his witty remarks. When I was two years old, my Papa Hilly planted a Japanese red maple seedling in my backyard. Over the years, as the tree's branches spread further and further into unmarked territory, I, too, evolved as an individual by delving into new interests. Fast forward to the present, and the maple tree continues to stands tall and proud in my backyard, not only serving as a symbol of growth but also as a constant reminder of the someone special who bestowed me such a precious gift—my Papa Hilly.

Papa Dave was a teddy bear. I would crown him as the world's best hugger, and I truly mean that with my entire heart. You could never escape his grasp, nor did you want to. You just felt so enveloped with love in his arms. When I was young, he began calling me his "little guy"— a nickname that he always adhered to throughout the years. Papa Dave had a hearty and contagious laugh. He was the leader and protector of the family, the man who sat at the head of the table and the one who you would turn to for wisdom. He had a deep fascination with trains, so much so that an entire room in the downstairs of my grandparent's home was decorated with train paraphernalia. One year, when I was little, I bought my grandfather a miniature toy train for his birthday. I wish I could adequately encapsulate in words the look of sheer happiness that spread across my grandfather's face when he opened the gift—pure joy. Today, the toy train is displayed on the table in my family's living room, serving as a cherished keepsake to remember my "big guy" with.

I lost both of my Papas, my rock stars, within a year. I was ten years old. I am often paralyzed by the fear that the memories of my grandfathers will slowly fade as the years ebb by, which is perhaps why I find so much solace in etching down all the memories I have while they are still fresh. Papa Hilly and Papa Dave played a formative role in my early development and beyond, continuing to influence my actions and decisions to this day. I am grateful for the memories of my grandfathers.

In the years following their passing, their absences served as a reminder of all that I had failed to ask when I had the chance. I never took the time to listen to their stories. I felt remorse of my inaction. To be honest, I still do feel this way. I know that, no matter what I do, I cannot rewind time. I cannot go back and ask my grandfathers about their world travels, the adversity they faced, or the lessons they obtained through experience.

However, it was during my initial years of high school when I came to the realization that I could use this sentiment of guilt for good—to ensure that others did not have to endure the same regret that I did.

As a freshman, I began working as a member of waitstaff at a local senior living community, Orchard Cove. I loved my role, notably because it allowed me to engage in fascinating, albeit brief, conversations with the residents. Through these interactions, I gathered tidbits of stories from their past. Yet, the narratives were never complete. I yearned to learn more. This desire to gain a deeper understanding of the residents' past sparked the idea for The Legacy Project.

In my junior year, I gained initial support from the community's leadership to pilot a program—coined The Legacy Project—that would encompass interviewing interested residents to understand their life experiences. Soon after, I developed posters to promote The Legacy Project as well as a series of approximately forty questions to be used during the interviews, which were crafted with the hope that they would generate conversation. At the end of the book, I have included a copy of the original interview questions, which you may find helpful to peruse. Within the first few days that the interviewee sign-up sheet was placed in the main lobby, every slot—including the waitlist—was taken. I was absolutely ecstatic to see there was so much interest from the community in participating in the project.

Twenty-two residents were interviewed over fifteen months. While the majority of them were conducted in person, the latter portion of interviews occurred over video calls when the COVID-19 pandemic struck.

Once all the interviews were completed, the process was far from over. Many of the write-ups went through numerous rounds of revisions, and all were approved by the residents themselves to ensure their stories and their voices were captured accurately. It is also important to note that all residents provided written permission for their stories and photos to be included in this book, and current last names were not included to protect each person's identity. Additionally, four of the original twenty-two stories were omitted from this book at the residents' request.

I embarked on the Legacy Project and wrote this book with three primary objectives in mind.

First of all, this project aimed to provide a unique platform for the residents to reflect on and share their life experiences. I concluded every Legacy Project interview with the question, "What do you see when you look at yourself in the mirror?" When asking this question, my intent was that it would provoke each resident to think deeper, reflect on their past achievements, and ponder how their own life experience has left a lasting impact on others' lives.

Secondly, I wanted to preserve the residents' stories for years to come for their families, friends, and fellow community members to treasure.

Lastly, I hope that this book will inspire others to take the time to ask and listen to the stories of their own family members. While I am a proponent of this message during normal circumstances as well, I believe the importance of connecting with others has only been intensified as a result of the COVID-19 pandemic. I urge everyone, especially members of the younger generation, to reach out and spark a conversation with their loved ones, including great grandparents, grandparents, aunts, uncles, cousins, and parents. Once this opportunity to connect is lost, it can never be regained.

As I was conducting the interviews, I was amazed that, despite the fact all the residents lived through the same period in history, their stories were so distinct from one another. Their remembrances were intriguing, as I could connect their personal experiences to events I had only heard in classrooms. I came to realize that a textbook account is simply one facet of a story that has many complexities. Talking to someone who has actually lived during a particular period in history truly provides an enriched, fresh perspective, which makes the learning experience come full circle.

THEIR LIVES REFLECTED

When I began this process, I never imagined the implications. I found consolation in listening and sharing the unique narratives of these special residents. Beyond learning lessons and preserving stories, I have developed close friendships with many of the residents, lending an opportunity to grow and learn from one another. For that, I am grateful.

I hope you enjoy immersing yourself in the life histories of these eighteen incredible individuals as much I did. Happy reading.

With love,
Arielle S. Galinsky

I. Neil

B orn in the heart of bustling Brooklyn in 1938, Neil spent seven years living in the city until his family moved sixty miles north to Beacon, NY. As the oldest child, with a sister Sheila five years younger and a brother Bert eight years younger, Neil found the age gap to be a barrier in developing a relationship with his siblings. Later in life, however, the relationship between the three strengthened. As a child, Neil understood the importance of family and establishing relationships. His father, Milton, always spread the message that his family should attempt to live happily, even when facing adversity. Later, having a family of his own, Neil never lost sight of this. As a child, the celebration of holidays often encompassed get-togethers with other families where each household would contribute by bringing food dishes. During his younger years, Neil found Thanksgiving to be his favorite holiday due to the inclusivity of the celebration with no religious connotation, as well as the overall relaxing atmosphere when all join together for a feast. Most of his family spoke Yiddish, and his paternal grandparents could only communicate in this manner. For this reason, Neil often read The *Jewish Forward*, which was written in Yiddish, in an attempt to pick out items from the news and learn new words through the process. At the age of thirteen, while living in Beacon, Neil achieved the Jewish milestone of becoming Bar Mitzvah. Neil was an active participant in many sports activities and played on a baseball and football team. During his free time, when his backyard swamp froze over during the winter months, Neil and his friends often played a refashioned form of hockey by utilizing large branches as sticks and a wood block as the puck. Besides engaging in sports, another cherished childhood memory was taking his sled to the top of a snowy hill and experiencing the thrill of going downhill.

With two younger siblings, Neil's role was often to watch over his sister and brother whenever his parents left the house—an endeavor for which he was rewarded. Beyond babysitting, Neil found work at the age of sixteen, serving as a waiter and busboy at a Catskills Mountain resort. With his charismatic personality as a teenager, Neil was friendly with all, yet found himself attracted to a friend group within the Jewish community. Possessing a leadership role within his local Jewish youth group, Neil would often coordinate weekly meetings and a variety of social events for the members. At the age of seventeen, he graduated from Beacon High School and, in 1955, headed east to attend college at Massachusetts Institute of Technology (MIT) to pursue a degree in electrical engineering. With a strong aptitude for math, Neil excelled in his college calculus courses. Yet, upon reaching his sophomore year, he decided engineering was not his desired pathway. Instead, Neil switched gears and studied industrial management, now located within MIT's Sloan School of Business, where he immersed himself in an array of management courses. This transition proved successful, for not only did Neil enjoy the classes he was taking, but he earned his place on the high honor roll his senior year at MIT.

After graduating from college in 1959, Neil's work was focused within technical companies. He worked at Clevite Transistor right out of college, taking on the role of a commercial engineer who provided answers to consumer questions relating to silicon diodes. In 1963, Neil undertook a new occupation as a general manager of light-measurement instruments at EG&G Electro-Optics, where he remained for the next thirteen years. Among other responsibilities, he took part in the development process of lasers.

Climbing up the ladder, in 1976, Neil became President of MATEC, where he oversaw the manufacturing of electronic components and witnessed the initial stages of fiberoptics. Finally, in 1996, Neil started his own business, Bernstein Financial Management, where he focused on clients' financial planning and managing investments. He retired in the year 2010.

Neil met his lovely wife of fifty-eight years, Sandie, in his freshman year at MIT while attending a party. She was two years younger than him. After dating for five years, in June of 1960, Sandra and Neil decided to unify through marriage. Just over a year later, the couple had their first child, Phyllis, in November of 1961. Neil prioritized his family over everything else. By working diligently throughout his career, he always ensured that his wife and two daughters were supported to the best of his financial ability. He explained how he never had an "unpaid day" for if he left a job on Friday, he would start a brand-new job the next Monday. The couple had their second daughter, Vicki, in 1963.

Neil and Sandie shared a love for sailing, especially when it was an activity they engaged in together. According to Neil, when he was forty years old, the couple "made the best decision ever" when they decided to purchase a beautiful sailboat. As their passion for sailing grew, so did the size of the boats in their collection. The couple's first boat was twenty-six feet, and their third boat was thirty-eight feet! For the next twenty-five years, Neil and Sandie ventured on numerous sailing trips in the waters near Cape Cod and Maine. After selling the boat at the age of sixty-five, Neil and Sandie embarked on numerous adventures abroad to over twenty-one different countries, including Kenya, Tanzania, Italy, Switzerland, Vietnam, Thailand, China, Japan, and Israel. While in Kenya and Tanzania, Neil and Sandie were "mesmerized by the variety and quantity of wildlife" and were genuinely amazed when a lion sprung onto the hood of their vehicle to doze. However, among all the trips they ventured on, one vacation in particular sticks out to Neil: Florence, Italy. Together, Sandie and Neil spent a month there, which, given the extended duration of time, allowed them to immerse themselves into the tourist attractions and Florence culture, as well as to wander off to nearby cities for leisurely day trips.

Neil stated that while he loves his two daughters and his role as a father dearly, being a grandfather is special because it comes with much less responsibility. As a grandpa, Neil's sole duty is to love his four grandkids, and out of that love, he helped support them through their education. Neil hopes that his "progeny and their progeny work hard to help solve global warming, religious extremism, racial prejudice, and wealth gaps and bear no ill will toward anyone regardless of race, religion or gender." He desires for the members of his family to advocate to reduce the inequities that divide people. When asked what his greatest accomplishment was, there was no hesitation to his response— his wife and family. Mournfully, Neil's beautiful wife Sandie passed away in 2018, yet her memory continues to live on.

A lover of concerts, reading, travel, theater, and lifelong learning programs, while in his eighties, Neil acquires knowledge and grows through his interests. He holds immense pride for his morality, as it guided him through life. He believes and adheres to the motto, "Treat others the way you want to be treated" and encourages others to do so as well. Neil desires to be remembered by his family as someone who ethically lived life and who prioritized family time. Beyond that, he hopes his children and grandchildren are aware of how much he loves them, and he wishes nothing but the best for them in whatever endeavor they take on. Most importantly, Neil hopes for them to enjoy life and take pride in their own actions.

II. Faye

Faye's childhood was unequivocally simple, yet delightful all the same. Born in 1926, she spent her childhood in her family's Connecticut home, dwelling alongside her mother, father, and two brothers—Harold and Robert. Faye's paternal side of the family arrived in the United States years prior; at this point, their Austrian last name, Koolak, was altered to the American name, Clark, at Ellis Island. When she was young, her father owned and operated gasoline stations, yet upon the arrival of the economic recession in the thirties, he was forced to maneuver to a new role within an auto supply store. Her mother, who was French born, arrived at Ellis Island in the late nineteenth century. She worked diligently as a school secretary in New Britain schools.

In her tender age, Faye relied on the radio for entertainment, as well as get-togethers with her friends at the temple. Her family often attended Friday night services at the local conservative synagogue. She enrolled in Sunday school courses, which provided her with an understanding of Jewish history. At the time, girls were not permitted to take Hebrew courses. So, when Faye was in her forties, she took classes at Hebrew College, allowing her to adopt an understanding of conversational Hebrew for her future trips to Israel.

At sixteen years of age, Faye graduated from New Britain High School in the top five percent of her class. She was forever grateful for the positive influence of her Latin teacher, who encouraged her to pursue higher education even though money was a barrier at the time. Without her and the inspiration she instilled, Faye may have never sought that path.

Following high school, Faye elected to enroll in a five-year nursing program at the University of Connecticut. She had earned a merit scholarship to cover first year tuition. Faye knew this program required students to work in the Norwich Hospital in Connecticut. However, upon visiting for the first time, she was taken aback by the facility's appearance. She immediately knew this was not the place she envisioned spending her time. After the completion of one year in the program, Faye altered her course of action.

At the time, society was experiencing a severe loss due to the deployment of troops and medical employees overseas to fight in World War II. The registered nurses that had once filled the hospitals were now taking on the role of heroes by protecting the soldiers wounded in war efforts. As a result, there was a shortage of medical personnel in American hospitals. The United States Public Health Service responded through the establishment of the Cadet Nurse Corps in 1943, a program that enticed young individuals to enter the nursing profession in exchange for full coverage of tuition to nursing school, plus room, board, and a small stipend. The Cadet Nurse Corps played a prominent role in American history, for it allowed for the successful operation of hospitals at a time when it was needed most. The Corps' legacy continues throughout history, as exhibited in 2020 when the governor of Massachusetts designated July 1st as Cadet Nurses Day and ordered a plaque in their honor to be placed in The Nurses Hall at the Massachusetts State house.

In 1944, Faye enrolled in the Cadet Nurse Corps program and began to work at Beth Israel Hospital in Boston. She tirelessly worked eight-hour shifts, six days a week. When the rarity of a free moment appeared, she could attend Boston Red Sox games free of charge if wearing her cadet nurse uniform. Because many experienced nurses were no longer in the hospitals, Faye found that she relied on her own experiences to learn. There were few exemplars for her and her fellow nursing trainees to acquire knowledge from. Faye admitted that her medical understanding at the time was less than profound, which sometimes posed a problem for treating patients. By the end of training in 1947, Faye took and successfully passed the nursing state board exams. At the age of twenty-one, she was a Registered Nurse.

Following this, Faye immediately took on the role of head nurse at Beth Israel Hospital, where she oversaw the other nurses assigned to her floor. In her third year of this position, a new opportunity came her way. In an unforeseen manner, the Nursing Director asked if she would take on the assistant teacher position at Beth Israel's School of Nursing. Despite her nursing training and Registered Nurse credentials, Faye did not feel equipped to teach others given she had not yet earned a bachelor's degree. Even when Faye communicated that she had no prior experience, her superior was convinced that she would do well. So, despite her hesitation, Faye accepted the offer. In her own words, "You do what you have to do sometimes." Little did she know at that time, but this position would forever alter her career path .

Yet another curveball was thrown her way when, shortly after taking the role as an assistant teacher, the primary instructor decided to take a leave of absence. Suddenly, Faye was put into a position she was by no means prepared for. At the age of twenty-five, she became in charge of the Nursing program at Beth Israel. She instructed courses for a few years and took a liking toward teaching.

As she was teaching nursing students, Faye felt it necessary to obtain a bachelor's degree in nursing herself. As the government would pay for the tuition expense, Faye decided to enroll in Boston University (BU). While focusing on her studies, Faye simultaneously dealt with the adversity of her own mother's death. During her last semester at BU, Faye lived at home to care for her mom before she passed away. She was grateful for her kind professors at BU, who provided her with exceptions to deadlines due to her extenuating circumstances.

In 1957, Faye received her Bachelor of Science in Nursing. She returned to teach at Beth Israel for one more year. Upon deciding that becoming a professor to nurse students was the trajectory she wanted to follow, Faye felt it was necessary to advance her studies even further. In 1959, Faye received her Master of Nursing degree, which was also covered under the federal government's funding. Faye soon moved to Simmons College as an instructor. During the off-season, in the summer, Faye also worked at Beth Israel Hospital.

In 1960, Faye fell in love with a man whom she met on a blind date. His name was Harry, and only a year after meeting, they would get married. He was an intellectual, incredibly strong in the realm of languages. Harry was fluent in six languages—Italian, Spanish, Yiddish, German, Hebrew, and English—which meant that language never served as a barrier during the couple's travels. During WWII, Harry was stationed in Italy, which is where he mastered Italian. Throughout their marriage, Faye and Harry often went to the North End in the summer months for the food festivals. The locals would often accompany the celebration by singing music in Italian, which Harry often partook in. He also loved the French language; anytime he heard someone speaking French, he would approach them for a conversation despite who or where they were. It was just the type of person Harry was.

In the summer of 1960, Harry often brought his mother into Beth Israel for medical appointments. Upon arriving one day, he paged Faye to come downstairs and meet his mom. Following a pleasant interaction, her future mother-in-law invited her to join their Rosh Hashanah dinner that upcoming fall. Faye went to the gathering and had a lovely time. She was well received by Harry's family, for after the High Holidays came and went, she was invited yet again to their Thanksgiving feast. Faye distinctly recalled Harry's mom pulling her aside that night, and stating, "In my day, when a fellow brings a girl to a family dinner once, that's it. You have been here twice already. What's the story?" When spring 1961 came around, and Faye was offered to join Harry's Passover celebration, she declined. His mother's words stuck with her, and she felt as if she was intruding as an outsider. Well, Harry quickly reacted. In March, he asked Faye for her hand in marriage, and three months later, she officially gained the title of Mrs.

Over Christmas break 1961, Faye received a call from a colleague of hers asking if she could help them with a great favor. Just like everything in life, when opportunity knocked, Faye answered. She was asked to go to the Peter Bent Brigham Hospital in Boston and care for the famed American poet, Robert Frost. Even though her winter break was time she hoped to spend with her new husband, Harry encouraged her to go. So, for a short while, Faye oversaw the care of Robert Frost and, through doing so, shared memorable interactions with him. Later in her career, Faye often shared this story when teaching classes. In her students' eyes, her impressive number of degrees, years of experience in the field, and the fact that she was a published author came second to the fact that she was the nurse for Robert Frost. Now *that* was amazing.

In Harry's family, it was the tradition for women to stay at home and not work. As a loving and respectful wife, Faye tried to adopt this lifestyle. First, she resigned from her professor role at Simmons College in 1962 and remained in the couple's apartment all summer long. Part of her time was spent writing a book, *Drugs and Nursing Implications*, alongside two other nurses. After a summer of incessant boredom, Faye knew this was not the lifestyle for her. It was not in her nature to spend her days dawdling. One day, she approached Harry and told him she was seeking a parttime job for the fall. Her mind was made up.

Harry only cared about his wife's happiness, and if working was her pleasure, then so be it.

Faye was inclined to call the Massachusetts Nurse Association to discover what opportunities were available. With their guidance, she was directed to the Catherine Labouré School of Nursing at the Carney Hospital in Dorchester. The school was in desperate need of instructors. After speaking with the Director of Nursing, Faye was hired immediately. She was a bit dubious at first to take the job due to her religious background. She was Jewish, yet it was a Catholic nursing school. The Jewish High Holidays were approaching, so, before accepting the job offer, she asked if it would be acceptable for her to take off days for services. The director was welcoming to her request, which drew Faye in. After working at the school for some time, Faye noticed that she interacted with the director, who was a nun, differently than her co-workers did. Faye always viewed the director as a colleague of hers. However, her colleagues had all attended parochial school, so it was ingrained with them not to act as friends with nuns. This difference in relationship placed Faye in a unique position.

Any time any of her fellow nurses wanted something from Sister Cecelia, the director, they would request that Faye ask for them. Because she was comfortable doing so, while the others were not, Faye bravely walked into the director's office and asked away.

For example, one year, there were classes scheduled on Good Friday. Faye found this to be shocking for a Catholic school. So, she sparked a conversation with Sister Cecelia, thoughtfully explaining why it was a bright idea for students and instructors to be given the religious holiday off. The director was receptive to Faye's view, perhaps because of how forthright she was, and the nursing school shut down on Good Friday. The only difference between Faye and her colleagues was she did not fear Sister Cecelia; instead, she saw her as an equal. Faye remembers watching her students being "capped" during the graduation ceremony while she, a Jewish girl from Connecticut, stood on the Holy Cross Cathedral's altar in Boston. It was definitely a sight to be seen.

Faye always got along with her mother-in-law, which was important because, in 1970, they began to share the same living space. After residing in an apartment in Mattapan for a few years, Faye and Harry purchased a two-family home in Milton, allowing space for both the couple and Harry's mom. Following three years of instructing in Dorchester, Boston University School of Nursing contacted Faye to see if she would join their teaching faculty. She seized the opportunity and soon became an assistant professor there.

At this time, nursing education programs began to transform. Suddenly, more and more community colleges began to offer two-year nursing programs, which would result in an associate degree and immediate opportunities for graduates to start working. This type of program quickly gained popularity among students, and Faye became intrigued. After six years of teaching at Boston University, she opted to switch schools. Faye landed at Massasoit Community College, where she taught as a professor for twenty-two years. Soon, she became the Head of Healthcare Programs at Massasoit, where her role entailed overseeing the administration of the Nursing, Human Resource, and Radiology Tech programs. However, teaching was where her true passion lay. So, for some time, she returned to her role as a professor. Finally, Faye became the Chairman of the Nursing Department at Massasoit until her retirement in 1992.

All the while, Faye continued to pursue her doctorate work, which she started years prior, at the University of Massachusetts Amherst. Because she was employed at a community college, the state covered her tuition for doctorate courses. Faye had completed all the required courses necessary for graduation, yet one crucial aspect was left: the thesis. She was enthusiastic about crafting a paper on the history of associate degree nursing. However, the process of writing a thesis brought many obstacles. She was assigned two faculty advisors at UMass who were to oversee her thesis's progress and provide guidance along the way. Every time Faye and Harry drove, for over two hours, to the UMass Amherst campus to meet with the advisors, they were always too busy to meet, despite the fact they scheduled meetings with her at those times. It was understandably frustrating for Faye, for she was so close to achieving the degree she had long sought. After stunted progress for quite some time due to a lack of direction, Faye decided she would not pursue the degree further. She was almost retired, and there was no longer a need. Thus, she took the Certificate of Advanced Graduate Studies with pride. Obtaining her doctorate was a dream unfulfilled.

As a diligent worker her entire life, for Faye, retirement was by no means a time for relaxation. Instead, she continued to learn and donate her time for the benefit of others. Faye enrolled into and fulfilled a one-year gerontology program at the University of Massachusetts Boston. She soon applied the knowledge she acquired by becoming a volunteer ombudsman. Within this role, Faye traveled to local nursing homes every week to interact with the elderly community. Her role was to ensure that the residents' needs were met and that no maltreatment was present. If an issue were to ever arise within the nursing home, Faye's responsibility was to intervene and if necessary, report poor conditions to the state. Faye was grateful to receive nursing home assignments who treated their residents with love and care. The Boston Globe did an article on nurses who became ombudsman, and Faye's picture was placed on the front page of their "on call" magazine. Throughout her twelve years in this position, she never once reported anything to the state. With a chuckle, Faye stated that she knew she had to stop volunteering when she began using a walker herself, as many of the residents were under the impression that she, too, lived in the nursing home with them! Even so, her generous spirit led her to continue giving back. Before moving to a senior community in 2014, Faye volunteered as a member of the Council of Aging and the Commission on Disabilities committees in Sharon, MA.

In 2012, when Faye lost her beloved spouse Harry, she considered the prospect of moving. She and Harry had lived in Sharon since 2000, and they were both members of the local synagogue, even before they resided in the town. Faye was involved with the temple's programs, as a frequent attendee of classes or a contributor to the lunch and learn series. Additionally, she served on the temple's board. However, upon losing her husband, the feeling of isolation began to creep in. Faye no longer saw the need to stay in Sharon, or by herself in a home. So, she started searching, and soon enough, she found the community she had desired at Orchard Cove. Within one day, her Sharon home was sold.

Throughout the years, Faye and Harry found pleasure in traveling together, which they did extensively. They often embarked on the Elderhostel programs in locations across the United States, which allowed them to concurrently learn through the programs they elected and travel to a variety of places for a brief period. They explored the rich artistic history within museums of Spain, delved into the lively street markets of Morocco, and traversed through sections of the Iditarod Trail in Alaska, among many other sites. However, if Faye had to choose her favorite among the bunch, then the choice was clear. It was Israel, without a doubt. The couple went together for the first time in 1968 and, after feeling right at home, sixteen more times after that. While there, they lived like the Israelis, not like tourists. The couple rented apartments or sometimes resided on kibbutzim, bought their groceries from the markets, and rode around on public transportation. One of Faye's closest friends from Israel was the Director of Nursing at Hadassah Hospital in Jerusalem, and the friend kindly introduced them to her physician and nurse acquaintances. Soon, Faye and Harry's circle of friends grew, and during ensuing trips, their newfound friends would take them out for dinner. Similarly, when the nurses and doctors came to the United States on sabbaticals, the couple reciprocated the kind gesture by taking them out. Because Israel was such a significant aspect of their life, in addition to her lengthy nursing career, Faye and Harry decided to donate an ambulance to Magen David Adom (MDA) Hospital. When Harry passed away, Faye also donated a Medicycle to the MDA hospital in her husband's memory. Many years after gifting this vehicle, a friend of Faye, who lives in Israel, reached out to her to share a story of a beautiful coincidence. The friend met two sisters who both worked as emergency medical technicians in Israel and who both rode in the Medicycle that Faye had donated. The interesting thing was the girls' last name was the same as Faye's.

Becoming a professor of nursing was never in Faye's plans. Yet, in 1950, a new opportunity came her way. She did not feel prepared, but she was willing to take on the challenge. Thank goodness she did, for that role at Beth Israel School of Nursing propelled her into a career of teaching. Faye found great fulfillment in her work, as it brought her so much joy daily. It is her hope that she bestowed that joy to every student she instructed. Even when Faye retired, the contributions she made to the world continued to pile. In line with the butterfly effect phenomenon, Faye's small act of teaching students likely led to the result of hundreds, if not thousands, of nurses who now applied this acquired knowledge to benefit others' lives. The tiniest of acts can lead to the grandest of impacts. Amid her entire career, Faye found her daily motivation by striving to be the best she could be, but her joy was rooted in her mission to help nursing students reach their potential. By the many lives she has touched throughout her career, Faye hopes to be remembered as a person with a kind heart who made positive contributions to the wellbeing of other

III. Carolyn "Hooky"

As a toddler, Carolyn often engaged in rounds of hide-and-seek with her father. While playing, her dad asked, "Where is my Hooky Dooky?" which is where her infamous nickname of "Hooky" originated. Born in 1919, Hooky adored where she grew up—Brookline—in the same neighborhood as the Kennedy family home. Often, Hooky and her siblings were mistaken for the Kennedy kids due to their matching sailor suit outfits. Family played an integral role in Hooky's life, as she was the fifth child born out of six, with two sisters and three brothers. Hooky and her siblings lived in their mother's home, where some of her most cherished childhood memories of playing with jacks or mumbly peg and climbing trees took place. Beyond that, when young, Hooky enjoyed skiing, sledding, and engaging in tennis matches. Living in a reform Jewish household, Hooky reminisces on the weekly Friday night Sabbath services that her family held. Later in life, after an ancestry review, Hooky gained a deeper understanding of her heritage by uncovering her Ashkenazi

Eastern Jewish roots and learning that her mother was fluent in multiple languages, including German and French.

Hooky attended a private high school, Beaver Country Day School, where she remembers being treated differently than her non-Jewish peers due to her religious background. She started her dating adventures at the age of eighteen, and within one year, she recalls she went on twenty-six separate dates! After graduating high school, Hooky pursued her studies at Simmons College on the pre-professional track. Following her graduation from Simmons College, Hooky ventured off to graduate school at Simmons School of Social Work for two years. At the end of her junior year of undergraduate school, Hooky got married for the first time to a man named Arnold, and later the couple had three children—Arnold Jr., David, and Doretta. While Hooky did not know this when young, she later learned that her first husband, was born on the same street she was. Arnold fought abroad during WWII, and the separation proved to be a challenge.

After Arnold, unfortunately, passed away at a very young age, Hooky remarried to Melvin in 1967. Upon doing so, the household expanded to six children—four boys and two girls. Not only did Hooky become a new wife, but with this large transition, she also immediately stepped into the role of a grandmother to a child named Arielle.

Hooky began her long career in a position with The Massachusetts Committee Against the Death Penalty. She conducted research that supported the prevention of this policy to be used in the legal system. In 1964, she later became Director of Heart Information Services at the Greater Boston Chapter of the Massachusetts Heart Association. In this role, Hooky served as a point person for individuals calling in with questions regarding cardiovascular problems and would often refer them to the proper medical site. Two years after taking on this role, in 1966, Hooky embarked on a new position as Executive Director of the Massachusetts Health Council. She dedicated twenty-two years of her career to this job, working to protect, promote, improve, and pursue individual and community health care. She spent lots of time in the Massachusetts State House, filing legislation on behalf of her organization. A natural-born leader, Hooky organized meetings with her employees, helped with professional development training for others in the field, and because of her generous heart, made lunches for everyone to accompany the monthly meetings.

In 1978, Hooky helped create the first hospice in Massachusetts, the Hospice of the Good Shepherd, and later, she helped found the Newton Senior Service Center. In 1985, Hooky was bestowed with the prestigious Massachusetts Health Council Award for her diligent efforts in the field.

Hooky was also one of the founders of the nation's first and only Public Health Museum in Tewksbury, MA, which opened its doors in the year 1994 and continues to exist today for visitor enjoyment. To rehabilitate the museum building, Hooky remembers calling upon local prisoners to renovate the space in exchange for good food and their personal fulfillment for doing a good deed. As the museum is located within the old Tewksbury hospital, Hooky recalls scouring through the collection of materials present on-site to gain history behind past inmates' records. She deeply immersed herself in the history of the hospital to ensure that nothing valuable was lost. Hooky's grave concerns within the field of public health inspired her to help found the museum. She hopes that, in the future, more students are inclined to enter the public health arena to make concrete change for the betterment of others' lives.

Melvin and Hooky moved to Orchard Cove in 2005, but Melvin sorrowfully passed away in 2015. Hooky, a grandmother and a great grandmother of many, enjoys sharing family stories with loved ones that highlight her comedic and lively personality. She is a lover of bridge and ping-pong, an avid walker who exercises every day with friends, and an enthusiastic attendee of the frequent educational programs on Zoom. Independence is in Hooky's nature. Thus, it is no surprise that Hooky recently moved to a new apartment within the community and managed to pack up all of her belongings primarily by herself. The community as a whole cherishes Hooky's yearly Christmas habits. On this festive day, she dresses up in Santa Claus gear and parades through the dining rooms with a "reindeer" in tow, distributing gifts to every resident and staff member in proximity. Since childhood and throughout her entire life, Hooky has been an avid tennis player. At 101 years old, Hooky continues to play the sport she loves so dearly.

Many years from now, Hooky hopes her family members recall her as a dedicated mother and a woman who loved them dearly. She desires for her loved ones to carry on traditions and pass on their heritage and history. She wishes that the stories she relayed to them are never forgotten, especially the ones that emphasized her comedic spirit. For example, when Hooky was younger, a relative of hers, who she described to be heftier in weight than most, came over to her home for dining. Throughout dinner, both Hooky and her family kept a slate underneath the table to track how much food the dinner guest ate. Hooky's witty personality is a characteristic she longs for her family members, friends, and loved ones to always remember about her.

IV. Fran

B orn in 1930, Fran grew up in a petite, yet cozy, apartment in the heart of Hartford, CT, with her mother, Rose, and her Bubby, Celia, both who came over to the United States from Belarus. Fran never knew her father well, for he sadly passed away when she was six months old. Thus, as she was the family's sole financial support, Fran's mother had to work diligently as a bookkeeper during the day and a typist at night. As an only child, Fran spent her time with Bubby Celia, who took care of her while Fran's mother worked. In hindsight, Fran noted her grandmother as the most influential individual in her life, for many reasons, but stated this was not something she realized until adulthood. Her grandmother was a wise individual who provided guidance to Fran, yet also offered her the space to be independent in her decisions. Celia was talented in cooking and baking, often listening to recipes broadcasted over the radio and recreating them from memory, rather than jotting the recipe or ingredients down. Regularly, Celia would communicate in what Fran labeled "Yinglish," or both Yiddish and English. However, she never learned how to read or write in the latter, thus providing her without means to write recipes in English on paper. Fran recalled a time when one of Bubby Celia's friends would visit the apartment every Sunday. The friend, too, could not write in English but wanted to send letters to her daughters living in New York. Thus, Fran would offer to write the letters in English for her, a kind gesture without a doubt.

Fran partook in a number of joyful activities as a child, including frequent outings to the movie theatre in downtown Hartford with her mother and grandmother. As a young girl, engaging with paper dolls was one of Fran's most cherished pastimes. She often purchased books that contained cut out doll figures and an array of clothes to mix and match. Playing with board games was another favorite activity. For hours upon end, she and her peers played a round of Monopoly, and often, because the tournament endured for a long time, they would put away the board intact and resume at a later time. During the wintertime, she enjoyed skating on a pond in the park, notably when the rink held nighttime skate events. However, upon reflecting on her childhood, her most treasured childhood memory were the occasional trips, with her mother and grandmother, to a farm that sold homemade ice cream (her favorite flavor being pistachio). At the A.C. Peterson's Farm, Fran would often go on pony rides, which she absolutely adored.

As she entered her teenage years, Fran worked as soon as she was legally able to. At sixteen years of age, she received her social security number, providing her the ability to secure a job. During her high school years, she took on a role at the local hosiery store, working as a sales clerk behind the counter. Fran remembered a specific day working in the store when two women walked in, speaking Yiddish. Because of Bubby Celia, who spoke Yiddish frequently in the household, Fran could understand the language well. The women, who were under the impression that Fran did not know Yiddish, began speaking poorly about the store's products.

Additionally, throughout her adolescent years, Fran was a member of a sixty-four-person glee club that was all-city, meaning it included students from all three high schools in the Hartford area. She spent an abundance of her time practicing and performing with this a cappella group. Fran also was a member of an all New England a cappella group, where she traveled lengthy distances to present with the other members in Brattleboro, VT, and Scranton, PA. Fran's singing performances did not end upon graduating from high school. Instead, she reconnected with this passion later in life.

While in a high school French class, Fran opted to involve herself in a pen pal program, where she was paired with another teenage girl, Marcelle, who lived in France. At first, they corresponded solely in their non-native language to one another i.e. Fran in French and Marcelle in English. However, they stayed in touch far past their school years, for they continued sending birthday cards to one another over seventy years after they were initially linked in high school. Marcelle and Fran met in person once as well. When Fran and her husband were on a trip to Israel and France in 1984, they spent a weekend at Marcelle's home in southern France, which was a lovely experience.

As a teenager, Fran related to her Jewish heritage mostly through social avenues, by becoming a member of a Jewish sorority. As a member of this group, she attended Friday night services weekly. With that said, her family was not particularly religious. A membership to a temple was not financially feasible; however, her grandmother maintained a Kosher household and observed Pesach's traditions. Growing older, Fran developed a love and pride for her Jewish culture. Her dream is for Judaism to survive long after her.

In high school, she also immersed herself in many traditional milestone events, such as junior and senior prom. Fran and her beloved husband, David, were high school sweethearts, even attending each other's dances when they were in their teenage years. Fran first met David at the age of sixteen while on a long weekend trip with one of her close girlfriends. She stayed at the Mabry Hotel on Ocean Beach in New London, CT, a lodging option accessible to many high school students at the time. One night, Fran was taking a nighttime stroll on the boardwalk with her friend when they encountered two boys from Hartford whom Fran's friend knew well. One of these boys was David. After a humorous conversation, the pair of girls and the two boys parted ways for the night. A couple of days later, David reached out to Fran to ask her on a date at a local stock car race track. Fran mentioned that she was less than impressed with how their appointment went. She thought that was the end of their communication. Evidently, David had a different impression on their initial date, for only a few days after the first date, he called to ask her on a second one. Fran was sitting with her mother at the time of the call, and to this day, she can distinctly remember what her mom said to her: "Just go on a date with him, Fran. It's only a date. You do not have to marry him." So, she went. After the second, came a third and so forth. Often, their dates entailed a walk to the local diner up the street, where they would converse over a shared packet of french fries. Five years after their first date, in June of 1952, Fran and David got married.

After graduating high school at the age of seventeen, Fran began her college studies. Sadly, soon after she did so, her grandmother, Celia, took sick. Fran's mother was often working and thus could not care for her. For that reason, Fran decided to depart from her studies and look after her grandmother. After three months, Celia's health stabilized, but Fran felt she had lost too much time to return to college. Instead, she began searching for a job. Luckily, Fran found an opportunity to work in an insurance company's payroll department, which she did for three years. Upon getting married at the age of twenty-one, Fran moved to Worcester for one year to live with David while he finished his last year at Worchester Polytechnic Institute. There, she was able to get a short-term job in the actuarial department of an insurance company. When David graduated from college, the couple decided to move, for a brief time, to the place where they both grew up: Hartford, CT. This was a temporary residence, as they were waiting for the finishing touches to be made on the home they purchased in West Hartford. While living in Connecticut for three years, Fran and David had their first two children. Kenneth was born in October 1953 and named after Fran's now late Bubby Celia. Soon after, in 1955, Sara came along, and she was named after one of David's grandmothers. In 1956, due to the growing family size, the couple decided to relocate to Natick, MA, where they purchased a home. It was here, in 1958, that the family gained one more addition—Gary, named after David's late grandfather. Fran believes that raising her three children is the most significant accomplishment she achieved in her lifetime.

After earning the title of mother, Fran focused most of her energies on the hearty task of taking care of her children. Later, when the kids grew older, she spent time bookkeeping for David's consulting business. Upon moving to Natick, the family joined the local temple, where Fran rapidly involved herself in the Temple Sisterhood by serving as the president twice. Natick had a chapter of the American Field Service, an organization dedicated to securing homes for exchange students in need, of which Fran also became the president. She and David also became parents to an AFS student with whom she is still in touch. Beyond that, both Fran and David were involved with the synagogue's choir. Every Wednesday night, they attended rehearsals in preparation for their performance on Friday evenings. Fran felt that singing was her outlet, allowing her to connect with others who shared her same interest. The married couple was in the choir together for over thirty-five years.

The couple's shared interests extended far beyond singing. They both loved to travel, and they did so extensively. One of the trips they embarked on was an adventure to Borneo, where she created unforgettable memories of wild orangutans and unique flora that inhabited the forests they hiked through. An animal lover at heart, Kenya was a special place for Fran, for she gained the opportunity to witness an array of exotic animals. She adored the giraffes the most. Over the years, she has collected hundreds of giraffe figurines of different sizes, all of which were gifted to her by others. With her children, she has explored Israel in its entirety through her multiple visits. In addition to those mentioned, Fran has ventured to fourteen other countries, including New Zealand, India, Cambodia, Costa Rica, China, and Thailand. Every trip they embarked on was well documented. Fran captured memories through photographs, which would later transfer to an album, and David frequently journaled to capture moments through words.

As years passed by, one thing that remained constant was Fran's love for volunteering and her desire to help others. Once her kids were grown up, Fran volunteered for five years at Framingham public schools, reading to kindergarten-aged children. She found it to be a delightful experience. After David sadly passed away in May of 2012, Fran attended morning synagogue services daily to recite the Mourner's Kaddish. On Friday mornings, the minyan always ate breakfast with one another after services concluded. One week, on a Friday morning, a man brought in a tin of muffins and offered them to the morning service attendees. This gesture inspired Fran to make a pastry of her own the following week, which she brought in for all to enjoy. From that point forward, she made an effort to bake a treat every Thursday night to bring to minyan on Friday mornings.

In 2017, Fran moved to Orchard Cove and quickly engaged in multiple programs and committees. Within the community, she continues to find ways to volunteer. Every week, Fran dedicates time to knitting small teddy bears and mice as a contribution to Project Linus. She serves as a dedicated member to the library committee and the hospitality committee, which welcomes individuals into the community. Fran also took on the leadership role as a representative for her floor.

When reflecting on her experiences, Fran believes to have lived her life with honesty and kindness. Those values were the most important to her. Her role as a grandparent to three boys—Jesse, Nadav, and Ilan—and one girl—Maya—is something she cherishes, for she could devote an endless amount of time to them without worrying about other responsibilities. When Jesse was only a few weeks old, Fran and David took care of him one day a week, often bringing him to the train store at the Natick Mall. She recalls how happy she was to receive the call from her daughter-in-law, asking if she would like to take Jesse for a day every week. Fran said, "As a grandmother, I was in heaven." Someday, she hopes to have great-grandchildren as well.

When asked what she hopes her children and grandchildren to always remember about her, she said "that I love them, that I am willing and enjoy helping people, that I would rather help than to be helped, and that I was independent."

V. Diana

A sense of community was always a vital component of Diana's life. Wherever she went, she found comfort in being a contributing member to a larger entity and connecting with those around her. This love for community likely developed from her hometown, Pittsfield, MA. The city was close-knit, so much so that Diana's mother and father knew all of her classmates' parents by name. Everyone knew one another; it's just how it was. Born in 1931, Diana grew up surrounded by her two loving parents and younger sister, Marcia. As a young child, and through her adulthood, Diana looked forward to holiday gatherings. The family always congregated to celebrate—her favorite aspect of the occasions. Every Thanksgiving, Diana's grandparents and cousins would haul from their New York homes to partake in a turkey feast in Pittsfield. The kind couple who helped with housekeeping and repairing damages in the family's home was also invited. Over the years, Diana's family grew fond of the wife and her husband, and eventually they became close friends.

Having immigrated from Israel to the United States when he was a young adult, Diana's father became the owner of a factory that supplied mattresses to local hotels. Her father was one of six, but four of his siblings remained in Israel for their entire lives. Diana and her father shared a tight bond; he had this natural ability to instill confidence within her. Exuding the qualities of care and patience was in his nature, making him a wonderful teacher to Diana as well. She considered her father to be one of the biggest influences on her life. As a little girl, Diana embarked on her first trip to Israel with her parents and sister. As they ventured about the area, her dad pointed out important landmarks from his own life, such as his childhood school and relatives' homes. When she grew older, Diana returned to Israel on numerous occasions to visit family members, but also to explore. Eilat's beaches were among her favorite destinations in the nation, yet she also loved the modern hustle and bustle city atmosphere found within Haifa.

She spent her elementary school years engaged in the traditional games of hide-and-seek and double-dutch. Monopoly was often a popular form of entertainment, especially when she grew older and began to play with poker chips as the prize. With a laugh, Diana stated that Monopoly taught her math; first, she counted the paper money, and later, real dollar bills were on the line. Diana often rode her bike to the local Sackett Brook, where she and her close-knit group of friends sat around for hours upon end, conversing over a picnic. When in high school, on Saturday nights, her social clique frequently joined together and danced to the melodies of Frank Sinatra, Bing Crosby, and Rosemary Clooney record music. Since Pittsfield was right near New York, it was a popular Saturday night pastime to drive over the border. In New York, the age for drinking was eighteen while it was a rigid twenty-one in Massachusetts. When she was old enough, Diana and her friends often went to New York nightclubs, her favorite being The Show Boat. Diana's parents pretended not to notice, even though she was certain they knew. When it came to dating, her mom and dad were strict and set guidelines for her to follow. For the most part, she complied. That is, except for one boyfriend she had who attended a Catholic school. They certainly did not know about him.

At the age of ten, Diana spent her summers at Camp Young Judea (YJ), a sleepaway camp in New Hampshire. When she was old enough, her summer job was serving as a counselor. There was something so serene about residing in log cabins and swimming in the lake, even though there was sometimes fright because of the leeches that lived in the water. Her camp friends returned year after year, making Camp YJ feel like a home away from home. As a teenager, Diana also worked at The Model Dairy, a famous ice cream shop that her father's friend owned. She served as a bookkeeper and documented money earned from the ice cream parlor sales. Later, Diana was embarrassed when told that her parents had to check over the books once a month because of how many mathematical mistakes she made. Diana learned an essential lesson from this: Monopoly cannot teach you everything.

At eighteen, Diana graduated from Pittsfield High School. Only a few months later, she began her freshman year at Smith College in Northhampton, MA, where she received her Bachelor's Degree in Political Science in 1953. Directly after completing her undergraduate studies, Diana headed to New York City to begin a three-year dual master's program in history and teaching at Columbia University.

During her first year in the city, Diana was introduced to the love of her life, Norman. Her roommate from Smith College knew him as her neighbor. She set Diana and Norman up on a date at the Penguin Restaurant in New York City. They hit it off right from the start, spending the entire night talking. From there, their relationship grew stronger and stronger. Nine months flew by, and Diana and Norman knew they were right for one another. Later, Norman's mother shared with Diana that when her son brought her home for the first time, she knew they would get married. Their connection was so special. By the end of 1954, they tied the knot. Subsequently, they purchased an apartment in Mount Vernon, NY, where they stayed for six months. Norman, too, was attending Columbia University to obtain his MBA, which was ideal because both husband and wife continued pursuing their degrees without interruption.

Their first home together was purchased in Port Washington, Long Island. Here, they raised their family and resided for over thirty years. After receiving two master's degrees, Diana started a teaching career at Mount Vernon High School, the school which her husband had attended. History was what she loved most, both to learn and to teach. To her students, she taught America's past as well as the history of Europe during the middle ages. For a year, she became a career counselor and found pleasure in that work. Because of her role as a counselor, Diana began to consider pursuing a future in social work.

Following two years of working in the school, Diana became pregnant with her first child and had to put her career on hold. Eventually, their family grew to five: Diana, Norman, their daughter Deborah, and their two sons Andrew and Richard. Diana felt content about her decision to pause her work, for she was grateful to have spent time with her children in their youthful years. Diana recalls a scary moment when her eldest child was learning how to walk. At fourteen months old, he had only crawled and had not shown any attempt to stand on his feet. One day, Diana took her toddler to the playground. She looked away from her son for a minute, when an individual next to her said, "When did your son start walking?" Diana looked at her with confusion, thinking that she was talking about the wrong child. Diana glanced toward the fence, and there her son was, on his two feet, exiting the gate and walking down the road. He was advancing toward the drugstore at the end of the street, a place where Diana would often purchase her son a soft pretzel as a treat.

When her kids were old enough to go to school, Diana transitioned back to teaching part-time. Rather than having her own classroom, she served as a substitute teacher in the Long Island public schools. Once, she took on a six-week substitute position teaching a group of boys who were training to be mechanics. It was a challenge to control the classroom and engage the students' interest, yet she enjoyed it all the same. The boys liked her as a teacher so much that they wanted to bestow her a present when it was time for her to leave. Mechanics was all these boys knew, so as a gift, they asked if she would like her engine "souped-up." Although she thoughtfully declined, she thought this was one of the kindest gestures. Diana always desired to help others, and she felt the best way to do that would be through social work. Her short time as a career counselor demonstrated that she could use positive interaction to bring welfare to others. She knew that the only way to make a prosperous professional career out of helping people would be to gain her Master's in Social Work. Taking classes at night, Diana worked diligently to secure her social work degree from Adelphi University. After a few years, she had earned it.

Once her kids grew up, Diana sought a new position. She hoped to dedicate her life to benefit others, yet she knew she had to make a living as well. During a conversation with New York State Senator Ralph Marino, she was offered an opportunity she could not give up. Diana had good relations with the Senator, for she had always supported his policies and campaigned for him in the elections. Senator Marino was interested in helping women prisoners find rewarding opportunities after serving their time to not fall back into the same poor habits. With the knowledge that Diana was a social worker, he asked her if she would like to spearhead efforts to help the female prisoners. He would find the funds to support her endeavors. Diana could not resist, for this seemed like an opportune moment. So, for the following years that ensued, she worked at the Bedford Hills Women's Prison, helping the women and providing them with insight and advice for life after serving their sentence. When an individual was scheduled to leave, Diana would converse with her and direct the prisoner to employment places with whom she had connections. If the woman also happened to be a mother, it was Diana's role to ensure her children's wellbeing was protected. Whether the kids were in possession of relatives or foster care, Diana was given the permission to meet the children at their homes and evaluate living conditions. Her work also entailed coordinating visit days for the children to spend time with their mothers. Within the prison, designated children's rooms were built to allow an adequate environment for these visits. It was essential to continue that connection, hoping that once the women leave prison, they could continue to build a healthy relationship with their kids. Diana's daughter, Deborah, began to volunteer alongside her. Evidently, the meaningful work her mother pursued left a lasting impression, for Deborah pursued social work as her career.

Through her work, Diana developed a friendship with her colleague, an ex-prisoner herself who dedicated her career to helping women prisoners find meaning. One day, the two ladies were driving together to work, when suddenly her friend says, "Diana, do what I say. Slow down and gradually pull off the road." Understandably, Diana was perplexed. She did not know why her friend made this request and could not seem to get an answer other than, "Do what I say, Diana." Her mind started to race. Was it a police officer? A fellow prisoner? Finally, she pulled off to the side of the road, and both women exited the vehicle slowly. Diana asked again, "Who was chasing us?" Her friend calmly replied, "There was a bee in the car."

Diana entered this role with the preconception that prison was a cold and brutal place, filled to the brim with mean people. She was happily surprised when she found that her stereotype did not meet reality. The employees at the prison were always friendly and did whatever they could to help the women prisoners. They wanted to help steer them toward a better life. Diana found her work to be incredibly fulfilling, as she provided direction to individuals who needed it and offered assistance to kids facing hardship.

Although they primarily resided in their Long Island home while pursuing their careers, Norman and Diana also owned a lovely second household in Martha's Vineyard and stayed there on summer breaks. They fell in love with life on the Vineyard and knew there was no better place to live post-retirement. Around 1990, Norman and Diana sold their New York home and moved to Chillmark, where they remained for the next twenty-five years. For Diana, the best aspect of living on Martha's Vineyard was the supportive community of residents that she and Norman became close with. Diana recalls the first few nights in her home with fond memories, for everyone was so welcoming and accepting. To emphasize, she stated, "If you moved to the island, the first thing you find is six people bringing you dinner to say hello."

Throughout their marriage, both Diana and Norman had engaged in many volunteer activities together. In Port Washington, she actively served at community churches and synagogues and helped to secure funding to open group homes for at-risk teenagers that had no other place to go. This love for volunteering remained constant in the couple's lives, even after moving to the island. Norman found his niche in mediation volunteering, while Diana became President of Martha's Vineyard Community Services, a social agency dedicated to creating a vibrant and thriving atmosphere for island citizens.

Diana also found a home within the Community Synagogue, which she became president of. Norman was the temple treasurer. Diana's role was to plan programs and ensure meaningful experiences for congregants, while Norman had to be mindful of money resources and allocate realistically. The couple was often teased for their playful bickering, as they would disagree on when and where money should be used. She coined themselves as the "comic relief" for the synagogue. Diana had been a synagogue member since she was a little girl, yet it was never because of her religious beliefs that she loved it so much. Instead, she cherished the community feeling of being a temple member and attending services every week. She felt as if Judaism bonded her family members, yet another source of community and love in her life. In Martha's Vineyard, the many churches and one synagogue belonged to one umbrella religious council. Despite the fact there were so few Jewish people living on the island, it was decided that one seat would always be reserved for a synagogue representative, ensuring Jewish voices are never drowned out. Whenever one member voiced a concern, all other committee members showed eagerness to help them. It was a beautiful representation of people from all backgrounds peacefully conversing. For a while, Diana was on that committee, representing her synagogue proudly.

In 2015, after a beautiful two and a half decades spent on the island, Norman and Diana decided it was time to move to a senior residence. At the time, Norman's health was on the decline. The Martha's Vineyard home was kept for their children, who now have found their community. They found a warm environment within Orchard Cove, and when Norman passed away shortly after moving in, Diana felt supported by the other residents. Upon considering her most prominent accomplishment in life, the answer arrives in her mind without hesitation. It is her three children and five grandchildren, who she hopes never lose happiness and accomplish their goals in life. While they have already positively impacted the world, it is too early to sum up the genuine difference each will make. Diana believes they will continue to do well all their lives. It is her absolute joy to spend time with and watch her grandchildren reach success. She hopes they always remember her as a truthful individual who never failed to push herself to be her best despite the possibility of failure. Beyond that, she hopes they know that she loves them so dearly. Diana is also a strong proponent for education, and if she were to give a piece of advice to young individuals, it would be to "study, study, study!"

VI. Zecil

Born in 1921 in Philadelphia, PA, Zecil received her name in honor of her late grandmother, Zysl. During her childhood years, she grew up in a traditional Conservative Jewish household with her parents and her two younger siblings, Wilma and Saul. From the first grade to ninth grade, she was an active attendee of weekly Hebrew Sunday School Society classes and proceeded to be confirmed at her temple. She enjoyed these classes so much that at the age of sixteen, Zecil decided to take training classes to teach Hebrew courses, which she did the following two years. She taught every Sunday for a salary of twenty-five cents, but over half of that pay was used to travel to her job.

Zecil described her childhood as fortunate, for her father's role as a successful physician allowed her family to enjoy a comfortable middle-class lifestyle. Zecil recalls the sweet memory of attending the movies every Saturday and enjoying hot dogs with a soda. She remembers spending much time with her first cousin Lily at her family's home in suburban Philadelphia. Lily greatly influenced Zecil's life by teaching her how to raise flowers and fruits, as well as distinguish poisonous mushrooms from edible ones when walking through the woods.

Zecil recalls a special four-month trip across Europe with her parents that they took in 1931, when she was nine. During this vacation, Zecil also traveled to Palestine to visit her paternal grandfather and other relatives. She thought it was remarkable to adventure throughout the country, visiting Haifa and moving through the lively street markets in Jerusalem. She relays how this trip played a role in her decision to join Hashomer Hatzair, a secular Jewish youth movement, at the age of thirteen. She had hoped to go to Palestine herself for this program before attending college, but instead, her parents influenced her to continue with her studies without pause. Zecil remembers a unique experience later in life in which she was on a train bound for New York City, and she heard a man next to her singing the Hashomer Hatzair anthem. After a conversation with the individual, she discovered he was also a part of the program, exemplifying the idea that it is indeed a small world.

Zecil studied at an all-female high school, known as the Philadelphia High School for Girls. After completing her high school studies at age sixteen, Zecil attended the University of Pennsylvania (UPenn) to pursue a degree in chemistry. Upon graduating in 1942, Zecil's father expected her to follow in his footsteps by entering medical school and obtaining a doctorate. However, she did not feel as if this was her destined pathway, and for that reason, she made the decision that best aligned with her own wishes. In 1942, the WWII war efforts were Zecil's call to action, impelling her to join the American Navy to play her part in fighting injustice. Upon asking Zecil why she chose the Navy over the other branches of the military, she stated that she was a fan of the blue uniforms.

She began working as a chemist in the Philadelphia Navy Yards researching fluxes. After seven months there, Zecil made the decision to join the Navy WAVES (Women Accepted for Volunteer Emergency Service) to venture away from home and experience the world independently in an environment other than Philadelphia. She was sent to Smith College for training in 1943, where she spent nine weeks focusing on drills, learning how to recognize various ships and airplanes, and becoming more adept at other necessary Navy skills. She served as Platoon Officer here, where she oversaw other WAVES trainees and led the group in whatever way she was instructed. At Smith College, Zecil distinctly recalls how her fellow WAVES trainees from the South would drink a bottle of Coke every morning before attending classes, serving as a wake-up call to how individuals with varied geographical backgrounds differ in their ways of life.

After this session, Zecil was one of the few women officers sent to the U.S. Naval Academy in Maryland, where she served in a chemistry lab with two other WAVES members. Notably, Zecil was the first ever Jewish WAVES Officer at the U.S. Naval Academy. She was stationed there for fifteen months before making the decision to leave. After her departure, Zecil returned to Philadelphia, where she was re-stationed to work in Secretary Forrestal's office as an expeditor. Her job entailed making over 100 phone calls a day to places all over the country to locate items or goods that the Navy desperately needed. In particular, Zecil is proud of two things she found for President Roosevelt: a white rubber matting to board a ship and a square tub to install in Airforce One. She recalls how this job as an expeditor connected her with a wide range of people and opened doors for new occupations. For example, the owner of RadioShack asked Zecil to open the first RadioShack store in Tel Aviv. She did not take this offer. Instead, Zecil was discharged from her WAVE duties as a Lieutenant at the beginning of 1946.

Zecil met her future husband, Sidney, on a blind date after graduating from UPenn. She recalls the first conversation she ever had with him. Sidney received Zecil's telephone number through a common acquaintance, yet he only knew of her nickname, and thus that was the first thing he mentioned on the call. Zecil was taken aback that a stranger would address her in that manner, so it did not receive the best response! With that said, Zecil and Sidney remained in touch through writing correspondence while they both actively engaged in the war efforts. At the time, Zecil served in the Navy, and Sidney served abroad in Europe, fighting in the Battle of the Bulge and taking part in the liberation of death camps. Upon Sidney's return from service to the United States, he reached out to Zecil to schedule dates. In 1946, they tied the knot. Zecil's Judaic upbringing instilled in her that it was essential to marry a Jewish man, which is what she did.

After an honorable position in the Navy, Zecil shifted to another role that was equally as important: becoming a mother. Zecil and Sidney had two children, Ellen and Michael, both who are successful and extremely established in their careers today. After having her two children, Zecil's focus shifted to juggling the many responsibilities that came with motherhood. For a while, she attempted to attend graduate courses at UPenn in the field of philosophy, but she decided to stop pursuing this degree as balancing both student and mother roles became a challenge.

By the year 1970, Ellen and Michael were off in college, pursuing their respective degrees. Zecil, a lover of the hot weather and the beating sun, relayed to Sidney that it was time to move to a place more prone to warmth. Thus, that year, the couple moved to Miami, FL, and Sidney continued his dentistry work there. In 1978, Sidney opened up his own dentistry office in North Miami

Beach, and Zecil oversaw all the administrative work at the practice until her husband's retirement in 1984. That year, Zecil and Sidney decided to adventure off to Florence, Italy, for a four-month paradise getaway, which was nothing short of incredible. They returned to Miami, and in 1989, they decided to relocate to Boca Raton, FL. Throughout her adult years, both in Philadelphia and Florida, Zecil was an active member of Hadassah and even served as chapter president and an advisor. She worked to raise money, educate, and run programs. Sidney and Zecil lived in Florida until they both reached the young age of ninety.

Upon landing at that point, they decided to return to the chilly Massachusetts environment to live at Orchard Cove, so they could be closer in proximity to their daughter, Ellen. Zecil is the proud grandmother of six, and great grandmother of five.

Notably, she is also a founding member of the Women in Military Service for America, and she took part in the efforts to develop the memorial in Arlington National Cemetery.

VII. Shelagh

This writeup is crafted using British English spellings to represent Shelagh's nationality.

The sound of wartime sirens, signaling the arrival of a German bomb raid, is one Shelagh has never forgot. When the noise blasted, Shelagh's mother instinctively grabbed her daughter's small hand and, together, they huddled against a wall wishing for safety. Almost eighty years later, Shelagh still recalls that empty feeling in her solar plexus whenever she hears the sirens play during movies.

Shelagh was born on December 29, 1940—a day forever remembered as the "Second Great Fire of the City of London," when the British city was tragically air raided by Nazi Germany. Hundreds of exploding bombs were dropped from high above, engulfing the city below in flames. Despite the damage that ensued, the brave firefighters saved much property, including the famous St. Paul's Church. The day following the raid attack, a now-prominent photograph of the church standing undamaged, yet surrounded by billowing smoke, "symbolized the capital's unconquerable spirit during the Battle of Britain."

Following her birth at the Nelson Hospital in Merton, England, an area known for its connection with the prestigious Lord Nelson, Shelagh spent the first months of her life with her parents in an apartment in Merton. Her father only had a few months to spend with his newborn daughter, for after that period, he was obligated to return to his role in the British army. Upon his return to service, he was initially stationed in the northern part of the African continent, and then later he fought alongside the Allies in the Italian Campaign. While stationed in Italy, her father partook in arguably one of the most critical battles of World War II, The Battle of Monte Cassino.

Despite this being one of the more costly battles of the Italian campaign in terms of life lost, thankfully Shelagh's father's life was spared. It was not by weaponry, as one might think, but rather a plain metal spoon. While sitting in the Army Mess for breakfast one morning, Shelagh's father, Jim, realized he was lacking a spoon to eat his cereal with. To retrieve this piece of silverware, he had no other option but to walk across the expansive Mess. In the moment, it was certainly an inconvenient task to have to travel a long distance for a trifling spoon! However, whilst he was making his way to the silverware, the section of the Mess where he'd been sitting was destroyed by an enemy bomb. All of Jim's colleagues sitting at the table with him that morning were killed. Because of its seemingly miraculous properties, Jim stored the spoon for safekeeping and upon his return to England five years later, he brought it home to give to Shelagh. She has yet to lose sight of this treasured spoon throughout her entire life, considering it as her most essential family heirloom that she will bestow to her son in the future.

Meanwhile, in England, it became extremely dangerous to live in Greater London because of the threat of attack. For this reason, millions of citizens were evacuated out of the centre of the city and dispersed amongst small towns or the countryside. Many older children were sent away without their parents accompanying them, yet because Shelagh was only three years old, she was sent to travel with her mother to a suburb of Manchester.

Prior to being assigned to the home of a sweet elderly couple, Shelagh distinctly recalls the massive theatrical hall in which she and her mother were required to stay on the first day of their arrival. For purposes of entertainment, people were asked to perform their talents. Shelagh's mother urged her daughter, a lover of singing, to go on stage, which she certainly did. For the crowd, she sang the famous war time tunes that she had practiced so frequently and, anecdotally, she was told everyone was delighted by her performance!

During the war, one could not find much in the shops in England, especially luxury items or heavily rationed foods. Every week, Shelagh and her mother would each receive one egg, one orange, and a two-ounce piece of cheese as their "luxury" items. The selling of toys was unheard of at this time, but thankfully, the elderly couple that hosted Shelagh and her mother, as well as their neighbours, often went far out of their way to create toys for young Shelagh. Perhaps the toy she cherished the most was the entirely homemade doll house, which was decorated beautifully with miniature furniture and electric lighting. To coincide with the house, Shelagh received a donated china doll, which was an absolute beautiful sight. It was one of her most prized possessions, for she was born amid the war efforts and thus never owned such a luxurious piece. One day, out of the love and excitement she had for her doll, she hurriedly climbed down the stairs to show it to everyone. While doing so, Shelagh tripped on the stairs, causing the doll to fall on the floor and break into a million pieces. Shelagh recalls the horror she felt as an eight year old upon realizing that her most cherished possession was ruined beyond repair.

Shelagh's father remained as a member of the Army until 1946, when he was eventually "demobbed" and sent home from

Greece. During the first six years of her life, Shelagh had little opportunity to physically spend time with her father, yet she felt his presence through the numerous letters he wrote and sent to her. These letters are something she will forever keep. She admired his desire to always write letters in an uplifting way, with fun pieces, drawings, and always ending with a mouse insignia. In those letters, he never discussed the horrors of battle.

Whilst her father was overseas serving, five- year-old Shelagh and her mother visited the home of some family friends, who happened to be owners of a recording studio. The friends encouraged, perhaps even insisted, that the duo create an impromptu record to send out to her father, who at the time was serving in Greece. The two of them taped a message on an alloy 78 record, and, if one were to listen to it, they would hear Shelagh singing all the famous war songs, a bit out of tune, and reciting lines from a theatre production she had recently performed in. Her mother was a bit "shy," so throughout the recording Shelagh often encourages her mother to speak up. After the record was complete, thankfully, it was decided it was too much of a risk to send it by post for it could have gone astray rather than reach the desired recipient, Shelagh's father. Eventually, Jim was discharged from the British Army, and, upon his return, heard the delightful record play. Shelagh still cherishes this record today, "which highly amuses her grandchildren" when they listen to it!

SHELAGH

As the threat of danger subdued at the close of the war, Shelagh and her mother returned from Manchester and moved into a small house, with a garden on the outskirts, in Wimbledon, England. When her father returned home from the war efforts, he joined them in the new home. During the time of living in this residence, in 1947, Shelagh's younger brother, Christopher, was born. This was a difficult time for soldiers, like her father, and their families, as the post-war conditions in London were quite dour, especially economically. No jobs for veterans nor government financial support were available. Far past the end of the war, perhaps even continuing into the early 1960s, there was widespread hardship and food rationing. Shelagh strongly wishes that all individuals, especially her children and grandchildren, living in the twenty-first century could get a glimpse of how "impoverished life was in England during the Second World War" and post-war. She believes this would make people get along with one another, merely out of fear of those conditions reoccurring. During the aftermath of the war, there were a few exciting events such as the marriage of Princess Elizabeth (now Queen Elizabeth) and Coronation, that Shelagh said, "cheered we Brits." She commented, "We all had to 'beg, borrow, or steal' a television for these glitzy occasions."

During the war, the possible threat of invasion by Hitler was always present, affecting the way that many British citizens conducted their day-to-day life. In particular, many Jewish communities were forced to "go to ground," and, even after the war had stopped, the presence of antisemitic perspectives were ubiquitous throughout England. For this precise reason, Shelagh's mother, Nellie, hid her Jewish heritage and customs to ensure safety for her family. In fact, it was not until Shelagh was thirteen years of age that she, unintentionally, discovered her mother was of Jewish ethnicity. When her lovely Uncle Phil had passed, Shelagh was present when a close family member handed her mother a Jewish prayer book. It came as a surprise to the young girl, for the greater majority of her life she had attended and even was confirmed into the Church of England. When she was older, Shelagh gained a greater understanding of her mother's past. Her mom, Nellie, was born in England, yet was also the daughter of two Jewish Russian immigrants who had been brought to England in the late nineteenth century with help from the philanthropic work of the English Rothchild family in assisting Jews' escape from Russia. Nellie's mother and father tragically passed away when she was three and sixteen respectively, thus Shelagh never had the opportunity to meet her maternal grandparents.

Shelagh's paternal grandfather had come from County Cork in Ireland, and her lovely paternal grandmother, Edith, came from the small County of Rutland. Shelagh shared a wonderful relationship with her only living grandmother, yet this was only after the war when her father would take her to visit Grandmother

Edith. Before that, she had not had the opportunity to get to know her father's mother. As Shelagh stated, "going to visit her grandmother was a real treat as she would always have tasty things prepared for her and had a home full of intriguing antiques, books, paintings, and a fabulous Victorian piano." As mentioned prior, during and after the war, England was an austere place to live. Thus, the visits to the home of her grandmother always felt particularly special, because Shelagh was able to indulge herself with the time she spent with her grandmother, as well as playing with her magnificent piano, jewels, or furs from the 1920s. Her grandmother Edith immersed Shelagh into the art of embroidery, by teaching her and then bestowing her a pre-war sewing machine on which she created Grecian style clothing for her dolls. Although Shelagh always wished her father would have let her keep more of her grandmother's belongings when she passed away in 1953, she still cherishes a few of her special clothing pieces, as well as a complete set of Charles Dickens' works.

Shelagh was also fond of her mother's brother, or her favourite Uncle Phil. Interestingly enough, he was born on a property in London, England, located on Forty Broad Street. Nowadays, any address in London positioned on Broad Street is worth an absolute fortune and is owned by some of the most prestigious banks globally. For many years, he ran the then famous Merton Park Film Studios and, later on in his career, became the Mayor of Merton and Morden in England until he tragically passed away in 1953. Within his role at the film studios, every year from 1948 onwards Uncle Phil coordinated a glamorous event known as "The Film Stars Garden Party." Because of their relationship to the host, Shelagh and her mother were allowed to indulge in the events' activities, which entailed engaging in Fairground rides and side shows in Morden Hall Park, alongside celebrity film stars. Uncle Phil also introduced little Shelagh to the renowned actor James Mason, who was so kind during their first interaction and even "bounced her on his knee during the filming of The Dark Lady with Margaret Lockwood."

In her young teen years, the statutory age to secure a job was fifteen. Yet, because of Shelagh's height, her mother encouraged her to apply for a position at thirteen to see what the result would be! Never having applied to a job prior, Shelagh "cold-called" numerous stores situated on the hectic Wimbledon Broadway. Despite the anxiety that came with applying to the job, the very first time she walked into a store requesting a job, she was met with a good response! The owner later telephoned her, offering Shelagh a weekend job in a travel agency for then just fifteen shillings per day of work. This is where she worked until the end of her secondary studies; by the time she departed, her pay had risen to one pound a day.

Shelagh had always been an ambitious student who had strived to position herself at the top of her class, and thus who took pride in her success in a competitive school environment at Pelham County Secondary School for Girls in Wimbledon. Year after year, she was publicly commended for her outstanding academic achievements. She credits her father, Jim, for helping her prepare for her studies as he would often work on projects with her or patiently and consistently quiz her on material in preparation for annual exams. One of Shelagh's proudest achievements from her young years was being awarded the national prestigious Beaverbrook Bennet prize for Commonwealth Studies at the age of eleven for her impressive research and final product on her chosen Commonwealth Country of Australia. Her ability to absorb information with ease earned her the nickname of "sponge" by her instructors, a quality she still wishes she had at the age of eighty. Whilst taking classes in her eleventh year of schooling, Shelagh joined a pen pal program and was paired with a teenage girl from Detroit, MI, named Suzanne. The two wrote back and forth, and on one occasion, Shelagh received a beautiful gift from her pen pal in the mail: a red leather wallet. She felt overwhelmed by this special gesture and prized gift, for at the time in England, there was still a dearth of luxury items available in stores.

At the age of sixteen, upon graduating from secondary school, Shelagh decided to enroll in a two-year hotel administration programme at Westminster Technical College, now known as Westminster University, to learn the ins and outs of managing a hotel business. The field of study was a daring choice for a female to take on. At the time, it was the norm for men to dominate the field of hotel administration, and rarely did women pursue schooling for it. Yet, aligning with Shelagh's ambitious spirit, she did and it took much perseverance on her part. Throughout the course, she had the opportunity to pursue three months of field work in hotel administration, which she took on with excitement. She spent her time in numerous places, such as the UK Trust House brand, The Dolphin and Anchor Hotel, and London's prestigious Ritz Hotel.

Working at The Ritz, as a female, required her to be persistent to earn the opportunities she deserved. In the 1950s, women employed by this hotel could solely be found in the department of housekeeping. Yet, with diligence, Shelagh managed to persuade the manager of the hotel to allow her to sample the work of each department to gain a full picture of the duties that were conducted. Much of her time at The Ritz was spent assisting the "stenographer," whom Shelagh described as "in her eighties, with long dyed orange hair akin to a Lautrec painting," and dealt with hotel correspondence. Throughout the reasonably brief time she worked there, she witnessed enough fascinating accounts to write a whole book! In Shelagh's words, she remembers "Paul Getty the first, who rented a single non ensuite room annoying the management by trying to cook on a primer stove! There was the famous Mr. Gulbenkian who arrived daily in his chauffeur driven gold plated London Taxicab and the old Aga Khan with his private amazing collection of wines held for him in The Ritz cellar, to name a few." She found the hotel kitchens to be "Dickensian" at best, with sawdust and grotesque rats scurrying amok, and the beautiful wine cellar to be best described as a "pre-war Aladdin's cave."

While taking courses at Westminster, Shelagh began dating a cadet, Barry, at the famous Royal Military Academy Sandhurst, where all the royal princes pursue their training. At the prestigious annual June Ball event, she accompanied Barry as his date in a gorgeous pink chiffon flouncy dress that she had been requested to wear by Barry's mother. Despite how distinguished the other attendees were by title, she was not so impressed by the "unladylike frolics she saw performed by many inebriated daughters of ambassadors." This relationship with Barry only lasted a short while.

Whilst working at The Ritz Hotel, Shelagh fell "hook, line, and sinker" for a man much older than her, who would soon become her first husband, George. Without a doubt, he was an exotic character that brought much excitement to her life during their relationship. He possessed the "charm of James Bond," and was an avid race car driver and collector of "comical motor" vehicles such as the Golden Docker Daimler and The Gull Wing Mercedes Sports car, now worth a fortune! The relationship was overflowing with constant excitement, for the couple often went away on weekend getaways. When Shelagh was twenty-one, she had her first beautiful daughter, named Alexis. When the marriage ended during Alexis's young years, Shelagh was obligated to return to work so she could provide for her daughter. Thankfully, her mother, Nellie, looked after the young girl.

She found a unique work position in the Bakery Marketing Intelligence Department at J. Lyons and Company, a business most prominently known for its tea shops and bakery goods. She was fortunate to be supervised by a wonderful Austrian Jewish manager who had worked for Britain's Intelligence Agency during the Second World War. During this period, J. Lyons and Company desired to enter the expanding patisserie market, which at the time, was primarily controlled by refugees from Austria and Germany who had fled due to Nazi invasion. Shelagh's job in the Marketing Intelligence Department was multi-faceted, for not only did she investigate the information contained within documents from the Economist Intelligence Unit and draft reports from her conclusions, but also she was a field "patisserie spy." She traveled around London, discreetly observing and recording the character of the sales at the other patisserie markets. During her time at J. Lyons and Co., Cadbury Chocolate Company also decided to venture into this market. As they would likely be a large competitor, Shelagh was sent to work for

Cadbury as an "industrial spy" to survey their new market and report her findings to J. Lyon and Co.

Following three years of work in the Marketing Intelligence Department at J. Lyons and Co., Shelagh married again to a man named Richard, a director of a family property company known as Rodwell, and she temporarily stopped working. She filled her days pursuing two of her interests—decorating the couple's London townhouse and carrying out charity work involving the art of modern dance. She found so much joy in modern dancing, often enrolling in hours of classes at contemporary dance master classes. As a volunteer fundraiser for the wonderful London Contemporary Dance Company, she chaired multiple annual gala events that raised a significant amount of money to go toward the company itself, as well as the school. In 1976, there was a massive celebration for America's 200th anniversary of the Declaration of Independence in London. Alongside many other renowned committee members, Shelagh worked to plan a celebratory performance featuring the Martha Graham Dance Company and was even bestowed a signed copy of a notebook by Graham herself! For the first time ever, the company performed at the Covent Garden Opera House—the true home of classic ballet and opera—in front of the Royal family! Over time, Shelagh also became a friend to Judith Jamison, a chair of the Alvin Ailey Dance Company, and speaks to the current chair as well. Although she began to pursue endeavors other than dance, her love for the art form remains strong, and she still finds ways to remain connected to her passion.

Shelagh remembers the numerous Friday night Shabbat celebrations she and Richard spent with his family. At the start of 1968, Shelagh and Richard had the first of two children, a baby boy named Jolyon, and in 1969, Shelagh had another girl, Eloise. Alexis, around seven at the time of her brother's birth, was a wonderful sister to both of her new siblings.

Shortly after they were married, Richard decided to sell his company so he could pursue two dreams: living in Israel and sailing his yacht. Shelagh was not content with the idea of moving to Israel at the time, for there was much conflict due to the Six-Day War and she did not feel as if it was an adequate place to raise her young children. Yet, Richard's dream to sail his yacht still persisted. Shelagh, a mother of three young kids, did not feel this was a realistic lifestyle and relayed to him she no longer wanted to be part of the marriage. By 1977, they were separated, yet the divorce was drawn out.

Simultaneously, in 1977, Shelagh moved, with the children at the time, from the family's home to a home overlooking the Thames River. She intended to "renovate the listed sixteenth century house on the grounds of Henry VII's manor house and joined to Paul Getty 11's Queen Anne house in historic Cheyne Walk."

Almost forty years after living in this home, Shelagh was watching one of her favourite television programs, The Crown, when, surprisingly, the facade of her actual Cheyne Walk home was shown on the screen! Shelagh learned that her home at 17 Cheyne Walk was where Princess Margaret actually met her husband-to-be, Antony Armstrong Jones! After Shelagh moved from this home, she purchased another property in Wellington Square Chelsea and lived there for seventeen years.

Following her divorce, Shelagh decided to return to work once again and entered the property market, yet it collapsed when the dollar went off the "Gold Standard." So, she found that it was a suitable time to return to schooling. Luckily, Shelagh successfully received a grant to enroll in the MIT Sloan Business Programme at the prestigious London Business School. Thankfully, whilst the children were still living with her in England, Shelagh hired a sweet, Irish nanny to watch the kids whilst she was at class. She is so grateful for her support, as she could not have otherwise taken care of her kids and pursued a pathway to her future.

Although Shelagh found the experience in the MIT Sloan Programme to be very rewarding, especially due to the fact that she was only one of two women, it was understandably challenging all the same. Her concentration was in behavioral science, and fortunately she had the opportunity to visit MIT's campus in Cambridge, MA, to meet the "early gurus of behavioral science." After her time spent there, the program required Shelagh to complete field work. For her, this meant working two weeks at Johnson and Johnson to evaluate their new management development programme. Particularly, the focus of the evaluation was ensuring the equal incorporation or involvement of females, especially those of colour.

It was whilst she was still finishing her courses at the MIT Sloan Programme that Shelagh, with her ambitious spirit, decided to begin her own business. Her enterprise would be known as Aston's Budget Studios. She began by purchasing two large Victorian townhouses in South Kensington, a location that would prove to be very accessible and desirable for tourists staying in the area. Although the homes did have sitting tenants at the time of purchase, Shelagh paid for them to leave. She specifically chose these properties, for it was already converted into small bedsitters that could easily serve as small boutique rooms in the tourist apart-hotel she had imagined. Interestingly enough, Shelagh opened the first tourist apart-hotel of its kind in London! Although Shelagh had a strict budget from which to build her business from, over a period of two years after the MIT programme, she was in ownership of the properties, the tenants were vacated, the homes restored to high quality conditions, and the rooms decorated in beautiful Laura Ashley fabrics. The rooms were bijou, yet comfortable all the same and held a beautiful appearance. Once the studios were ready for consumers to stay in, Shelagh marketed her unique product to, predominantly, American and Japanese tourist markets and traveled across the globe to do so. To her amazement and pleasure, the business was a booming success! One of Shelagh's good friends kindly introduced her to the authors of the Frommer's guide books, a best-selling travel book guide, who was overwhelmed by Shelagh's enterprise brand and loved the new concept of "Aston's Designer Studios." For many years consecutively, Shelagh's business—Aston's—was written up as the "Best Value London hotel."

In 1982, Shelagh married once more to a man named Philip. Her business was truly booming at this time, which of course occupied her time significantly. However, during slower periods of the year, Philip and Shelagh loved to engage in travel with one another. Out of the annual trips they made, Italy was the place she cherished the most. Shelagh enjoyed her time at the Excellsior Hotel in Florence, lending the breathtaking view of the River Arno and Ponte Vecchio.

Throughout the twenty-five years she operated her business, Shelagh had to purchase a third townhouse to meet demand for her product. In 1997, she decided to sell her lovely business that she had developed from the ground up. During this transition period of her life, her home in Wellington Square was also sold, allowing her to purchase and entirely renovate a stunning villa on the Mediterranean Sea, bordering France and Monaco. Shelagh also kept an apartment in London, allowing her to travel back and forth if she desired.

By 2002, Shelagh and Philip were no longer together. Yet, this was the year she met her wonderful last partner—Keith—who had "established a charity for survivors of torture." During the nine-year period they dated and lived with one another, Shelagh survived cancer of the throat and was subject to harsh treatments at an oncology facility in London. She felt supported by many during this time, including Keith and her wonderful friend Liz who tragically later died from cancer herself. Once she entered remission, Shelagh had endured a lot throughout her fight with cancer. Traveling from her villa in Cap d'Ail to her Kensington, London, apartment was no longer a feasible undertaking. Thus, she opted to live solely in her French villa, although she will always consider herself a "True Brit."

Despite the luxurious and relaxing lifestyle that coincided with living on the Mediterranean Sea, Shelagh longed to spend time with her children and three grandchildren, all who resided in America. There was no more family time to be lost. In 2017, Shelagh moved to another continent—America—to live nearby her eldest daughter and son in a senior community.

As Shelagh said, she "adores her three lovely grandchildren, Tadus, Ellis, and Laila." Upon considering what her most significant accomplishment was in life, without hesitation, she said "her three children." In her words, she believes her "children and grandchildren are special, lovely people who contribute goodness to the world...what more could their English mother and grandmother want!" Shelagh also remains close to her brother Chris and his wife Diane. While they are separated in distance, Shelagh living in America and Chris in Devon, England, they remain in constant communication.

When asked what she hopes her three grandchildren will remember about her, she said "their English grandmother, who was an ambitious business builder who loved the arts and who built up what she had from little resources." Beyond that, she said, she hopes they remember that "she loves them infinitely."

VIII. Joan

Joan, and her husband, Larry, shared an enthusiasm for an unusual pastime: waking up at the crack of dawn to view the sun rising. Throughout their long fifty-six-year marriage, this is an activity they cherished spending with one another. Joan reminisces on the first date she shared with her future husband when she was twenty-two years old, when Larry asked her to attend a production with him at a New York City theatre. After the play was over, they headed over to Greenwich Village to enjoy conversation and sweet pastry. In Joan's words, there was unquestionably some chemistry between the two of them. This relationship continued until 1959, when the couple decided to solidify their connection with marriage.

After completing her high school studies in 1954, Joan ventured off to Perth Amboy General Hospital School of Nursing in New Jersey, where a full scholarship was awarded to her to complete her academic courses. Entering nursing school was also her first opportunity to live independently. Joan gained her nursing license in 1958, which she then put to use soon after. While still residing in New Jersey, Joan spent her days working in the Perth Amboy General Hospital as a nurse for patients preparing and recovering from surgery. Yet, even after gaining her license for nursing, Joan felt it was imperative to continue her learning and add an undergraduate degree to her curriculum vitae. She initially enrolled in part-time credit classes at Rutgers University and began embarking on this degree. Additionally, while living in New Jersey, Joan and Larry had their first child, David, in 1960 and their second child, Ellen, in 1962.

In 1965, Joan and Larry decided to move to Sharon, MA, to raise their family, where they proceeded to reside for the next fifty years. While in Massachusetts, Joan had her third and final child, Robert, in 1966. She focused the majority of her energy on the essential and time-consuming duty of motherhood, ensuring she was always present in the lives of her three children. Additionally, during this time, she spent hours volunteering in classrooms and answering calls, alongside Larry, at a self-help hotline. Joan continued to pursue her undergraduate studies through part-time classes, where she focused on the social sciences, at Harvard Extension School.

After twenty years of engaging in part-time courses, Joan succeeded in earning her bachelor's degree. Even so, she was still not satisfied. She was driven to climb higher. With the desire to continue to achieve her master's degree, as well as with the understanding she did not have twenty more years to do so, Joan enrolled and completed a full-time master's program, at what is now called Lesley University, in counseling in 1979. Securing this degree set the stage for the rest of her career.

After graduating, Joan's first opportunity was working with a population of financially unstable, psychologically ill individuals in a state-owned hospital in Dorchester, MA. While she had enjoyed this position, as well as working with this patient population, she only stayed a year due to a frightening encounter she endured while walking in the vicinity of the workplace. While strolling down the street one day on her way to work, an individual approached her and demanded the possession of her car keys. Thankfully, she remained safe through this interaction, yet this experience served as Joan's call to action to seek new job opportunities elsewhere.

The job search landed her a role at a Catholic organization, The House of Affirmations, where she would engage with nuns, priests, and brothers who were in need of a therapeutic community. Joan called upon her memories of her job interview, admitting that she felt the need to be completely transparent and reveal her Jewish heritage to the interviewer. To her delight, the job interviewer demonstrated acceptance for her Jewish background and relayed to her that religious diversity would be a sublime thing to expose the clients to. Joan was passionate about her role and cared greatly for her clients. Every so often, she would attend special Mass services to demonstrate support for her clients, especially when her clients' work would be celebrated in some capacity on these occasions. She greatly enjoyed her time at The House of Affirmations, and she did not depart from this role until the organization folded in the late 1980s.

At that moment in her life, Joan was at a crossroads. She could reinitiate the job-seeking process, or she could choose the road less traveled and embark on a new adventure. After looking for work, Joan determined that this was not the direction she wanted to take. Instead, this was the perfect opportunity to continue her education and pursue a second master's degree, this one in social work. In 1990, Joan enrolled in the program offered by Smith College, and two years later, she completed this enlightening academic experience.

This experience propelled Joan to take a job in the Massachusetts prison system, where she worked at the MCI Norfolk facility and Pondville Correctional Center. She found pleasure in working with the inmates, both at the individual and group level, as well as focusing on crisis intervention. Joan discovered satisfaction and fulfillment within her work, for she had the unique opportunity to help others, especially those who desperately wanted to turn their lives around for the better. Through her conversations with inmates, Joan contributed significantly to the self-repair and reflecting process within these individuals. After ten years in this role, at the age of seventy-four, Joan decided to step away to focus more of her time with her husband, Larry.

Joan is grateful for the numerous travel experiences that she embarked on with Larry. Upon being asked what her favorite destination was, Joan replied without pause—Paris. She remembers the sweet sight of the Arch of Triumph, the beauty of the Eiffel Tower, and the wonderful feeling she experienced when sitting in the outdoor cafés surrounded by the lull of the beautiful French language. She cherishes the memories of her fourth Paris trip, when Larry traveled to the local bakeries every morning to retrieve freshly baked baguettes for breakfast.

Upon Larry's passing in 2015, Joan decided that it was best to move into a community that she had so long wished to be a part of: Orchard Cove. She has found her home, and she is content with the welcoming and supportive group of individuals that reside there. Even while living in this community, Joan continued to take the time for herself to travel. She recalls relaxing on a cruise boat deck en route to Bermuda, where she enjoyed the serene atmosphere of ocean waves bobbing up and down. Before heading to the Berkshires for a vacation, Joan filled her itinerary with destinations to go to, including the theatre, Tanglewood, and museums. In 2016, Joan decided to go to her most beloved vacation spot, Paris, one last time. This trip proved to be an unforgettable experience. She recalls being the oldest, yet most energetic, individual on the journey, for she walked a mile or so every day without complaint.

At the age of eighty-five, Joan has found so much joy in life. Despite barriers that have come her way recently, she said, "Life is still good!" with a beaming smile on her face. Over the past few years, she discovered a keen interest in creative writing through a workshop. After crafting many written creations, with some support, Joan self-published her pieces. She also has drafted articles to publish in The Gazebo, Orchard Cove's own newspaper.

When asked what her most prominent accomplishment was in life, Joan was quick to answer that it was bringing her kids and, indirectly, grandkids into this world. She feels proud to have provided the world and its communities with such good people. As for what she wants her kids to always remember about her, well, that answer was quite simple. In the words of Joan, her reply was "that I love them."

IX. Geri

Geri, born in 1934, was the proud daughter of two immigrants, Joseph and Gussie, who arrived at Ellis Island from Russia. Despite their European roots, her parents quickly became accustomed to the American traditions and way of life. Gussie came to the United States when she was just a little girl, with her mother and four siblings. As a family, they opened up a bed and breakfast in the Lower East Side of New York City, where Gussie, as well as her sisters and brothers, worked. Because it was a familial effort to keep the business operating efficiently, Gussie never had the opportunity to pursue higher education. Thus, she strongly advocated for her two daughters, Geri and Selma, to pursue education past grade school so they could have the academic experience that she was deprived of. That, Geri and her sister certainly did.

During her childhood, Geri's family observed Conservative Judaism. They would often go to synagogue on the High Holidays and they kept a Kosher home for many years. Geri was a frequent attendee of Hebrew and Sunday School, yet she never felt connected to the teachings. Thus, as Geri grew up, she distanced herself from the Jewish heritage and holidays, and instead, she placed more importance on family traditions. As a result, in her adult years, her favorite holiday became Thanksgiving because it allowed everyone to convene as a family.

Her childhood years were spent in Buffalo, NY, initially in the upstairs unit of a two-story family home. Her father owned a dress shop, located only a few blocks away from their residence. Geri often walked to her father's store, and along the way, stopped at the penny candy shop to purchase sweets. While her mother did not work during Geri's toddler years, Gussie joined her husband in the store when Geri went to school. Gussie was responsible for frequent trips to New York City, where she selected the store's merchandise. Some of the best memories from Geri's young years were within her dad's store, for she would spend time trying on all of the new dress arrivals. He was a talented, and entirely self-taught, tailor who, at times, made clothes for Geri. Once, he created her a beautiful red, white, and blue tutu out of crepe paper and lined with silk for her to fashion at a Halloween party.

Later, her family moved to a home in the suburbs. There, she attended the local elementary school, which possessed a racially and ethnically diverse student body. The school's music teacher brought the idea of a "Festival of Lights" to fruition, by coordinating a schoolwide event celebrating the winter holidays of all religious backgrounds. At the time, this was a new idea entirely. Even so, not everyone in her town was accepting of differences. As a child, kids in the neighborhood often chased Geri home from school, threw snowballs, or shouted horrific names due to her Jewish background. It was her first encounter with antisemitism and, frankly, hatred in any form. Her childhood experiences perhaps played a role in how passionate she was, later in life, to fight for peace among all. If given one problem to solve, Geri would make peace everlasting in the world. She wishes that people would stop finding faults in one another, and rather, let everyone be who they are.

During her young years, she explored many interests, such as roller-skating, bike riding, or playing games like curb ball. She particularly favored spending her time with paper dolls, which she dressed and made clothes for. Her artistic talents were not limited to this realm, however. She found her love for coloring and painting as well. These were hobbies she carried into adulthood. As a teenager, she often had to do whatever she could to help around the home. Geri remembers her mother as an exceedingly neat and strictly clean individual. Every week, Gussie moved all the furniture, piece by piece, out of each room, which would allow her to clean all the floors in their entirety.

91

GERI

Geri helped with cleaning the home, washing dishes, and going to the store to fetch things her mother needed for cooking. Her parents, two very conservative individuals, always laid strict rules for their daughters to follow. However, Geri was reasonably rebellious. She took a different path, one that did not always abide by her parents' wishes. She valued the time with her friends on weekend nights, and thus, she would come home whenever she desired, taking the consequences that came with the choice. For Geri, it was essential to make her own decisions. This message rang true her entire life. When something bothered her, Geri responded by tapping into her own strength, establishing her independence, and sticking up for herself. The importance of being in control of her own decisions was one of the most fundamental lessons she has ever learned.

Her father, Joseph, was a man liked by everyone he came across. He was notoriously quiet and very relaxed, so "when he had something to say, you knew it was important." Although Geri's mother did not always approve of her daughter's decisions, Joseph demonstrated his support. He would pull Geri aside, telling her that if she felt strongly about something, she should pursue it. Geri remembers her father as a "very sweet man."

Throughout her grade school years, Geri always had a boyfriend. From second grade onwards, she could not help but find herself in love. Throughout high school, Geri often attended dances on

Saturday nights at the local Jewish center. This type of social gathering is where she met her husband at the age of fourteen. During one event, he asked her to dance. Later, he invited her to spend New Year's Eve together at a friend's party. Their relationship bloomed from this point onward. After five years of dating, Geri and her husband got married in June 1954, once he completed his first year of medical school.

Despite facing difficulties during her pregnancies, Geri was blessed to have four healthy children: Amy, Richard, Elizabeth, and Wendy. In 1959, the family moved to Boston, as that is where her husband had completed his medical school residency. For many years of her life, her role was to serve as a stay at home mother and a doctor's wife. Geri prized her children and cherished the opportunity to watch them grow. Yet, she also knew she wanted something more. When her youngest child, Elizabeth, entered the first grade, Geri woke up one morning and said to herself, "Is this all there is?" This question prompted her to seek a job for herself.

Before marriage, Geri spent time working at a doctor's office and found an interest in that role. For this reason, she thought an opportunity in the healthcare industry would be a fitting place to reinitialize her career. Thus, Geri began working at a small medical center—Robert Breck Brigham Hospital—where she worked with a team of friendly individuals. Following this, she headed over to Children's Hospital and found a position working for one of the practicing physicians. During this time, as she had not pursued her undergraduate degree prior, Geri enrolled in courses at Northeastern University in Boston. Not only did she successfully complete the classes, but she also excelled in them. Working at Children's conferred benefits, for they covered the majority of tuition costs to allow employees to pursue higher education. She continued to take classes. Geri felt compelled to search for more senior ranking jobs in the health care field. Often, Geri would be one of the final applicants, but because of her lack of a degree, the hiring agents had to eliminate her from the pool. This frequent rejection was Geri's call to action.

At this point, Geri and her husband had collectively decided, after twenty-three years of marriage, to separate from one another due to a growing difference in their life interests. They moved near each other so the kids could switch homes every other week, which allowed Geri the opportunity to spend time with her children but also to pursue her studies and date. She knew that securing an undergraduate degree would take too much time, time that she merely did not want to waste. Beyond that, she was aware that an undergraduate degree would not get her anywhere, and instead, a master's was necessary. A colleague of hers recommended approaching the Boston University (BU) School of Public Health Dean to ask if they would consider her for admission based on her extensive experience and studies. She had to work up the courage to do this because she was often timid when difficult choices faced her. She eventually overcame this fear by abiding by the motto of "biting the bullet" and tackling what frightened her head on. Geri walked into the BU School of Public Health with a question and she left with a mission. She was told to take the Graduate Record Examinations (GRE) and return after doing so. So, she began studying.

Upon achieving a good score on the exam, BU's School of Public Health accepted Geri into the program on probation until she successfully completed four courses. She dedicated herself to her studies and graduated with a Master of Public Health degree in 1984. Obtaining her master's opened up numerous opportunities that were not accessible before. She became the manager of multiple research departments at Boston hospitals, including Brigham and Women's, Beth Israel Deaconess, and Dana Farber Cancer Institute. She felt grateful for the number of outstanding individuals she interacted with through her roles, including physicians, lab technicians, Ph.D.s, and outside professionals who visited the lab. She possessed an enthusiasm to wake up every morning and go to work, for she knew how important her role was. Geri helped facilitate the research occurring within the labs, which in the future, would lead to greater scientific understanding and ultimately improve lives. Her work was meaningful, which kept her driven, and she loved it thoroughly. Geri dedicated the rest of her career to managing labs. It was not until she moved to Orchard Cove, in 2018, that she elected to retire.

Sailing had always piqued Geri's curiosity. As a child at camp, she took a few sailing instruction courses, yet she did not seek it further until adulthood. She became a member of the Pelagic Sailing Club, where all that was required of her was a twenty-five dollar annual fee. This club offered boat owners a place to secure necessary crew members. It was a mutually beneficial situation. Geri, driven by her interest in the art of sailing, became crew on many cruises. She reflects upon her sailing journeys with fondness. The boat she traveled on, the destination, and the other crew members changed frequently, but what remained constant was the communal and joyful atmosphere of her trips.

All crew pitched in with meals, by bringing various ingredients on the boat and cooking for one another. On two occasions, Geri embarked on unforgettable sailing trips to the Greek Islands and the Grenadines. Every night, the five-person crew, captain, and the members on the other boats would spend the night on the closest island, eating with one another, and celebrating with cocktail hours. Geri also took a week sailing trip to Maine, along with a couple, which was an experience she relished. As luxurious as it sounds, sailing is no easy undertaking. According to Geri, there is always a lot to do as a crew member.

Upon considering who has influenced her life the most, Geri found it difficult to limit it to one or even a few individuals. As an active advocate for the 1970s women's rights movement, she believes that many of her fellow feminists inspired her. Geri read the books and publications that sparked the national campaign, written by distinguished leaders like Gloria Steinem and Betty Friedan. This opened her eyes to how repressed women were throughout history, often with their voices ignored. Sparked by the injustices faced by women, Geri took an active role in the feminist movement. Yet, this cause was not the only thing Geri protested for, for she was also heavily involved in the peace movement that occurred during the Vietnam War. Geri joined the Women's Peace and Freedom Movement, where she came across many magnificent individuals who taught her a number of lessons. Once, Geri, among others, went to a Harvard University graduation ceremony to distribute peace information pamphlets. She recalls how adverse the reactions were, such as how some individuals responded by spitting on her. Despite the poor treatment, Geri is a firm believer of sticking up for causes she deeply cares about. For her, ensuring peace was undoubtedly one of those things.

Although her involvement in protests had long ceased by the time she moved into Orchard Cove, Geri stated that "her heart is still there." She believes that the most important thing is to educate yourself and be aware of the world around you. Geri encourages individuals to take heed of all perspectives, rather than listening to one person's viewpoint, as this type of approach allows for educated decisions to be made. Throughout her entire life, Geri proudly exercised her right to vote, and she encourages all to do the same.

Geri appreciates her family and highlights the love she possesses for them. Her favorite thing about being both a mom and a grandma to six grandchildren is one and the same—when they were growing up, she was eager about where they would end up in their futures. When her kids were little, she spent time imagining what careers they would venture into upon becoming adults.

She watched her children grow up to be successful in their endeavors, but also follow their passions. Elizabeth, a lover of cooking ever since she was little, went to culinary school, and now works as the head chef, overseeing others, under a national company. Amy became a social worker, then a nurse, and then decided to become a licensed nurse practitioner for patients suffering from addiction. Richard worked at the Boston Globe newspaper for over twenty years, becoming the assistant editor of the entertainment section, and continued his work in other areas of the public relations industry. Her other daughter, Wendy, is a computer design artist. Geri enjoyed watching her children start their careers, and she continues to find excitement in watching her grandchildren do the same. Geri states that her most significant accomplishment, alongside her education, was having four children who developed into honest and wonderful human beings. Geri expressed, "Any time you bring a good person into the world, it is a good thing." By her family, she hopes she is always thought of as someone who cared for them dearly and exuded goodness into the world.

X. Irene

Born on the 28th of February in 1928, Irene grew up in Dorchester, MA, with her parents and sister, Janice. Irene's father, a doctor, opened his general practice in the city and often took care of patients through house visits. The majority of her summers were spent in Woodstock, VT, at her grandparents' home, where she would often swim in the local brook or adventure on bike rides throughout the community. When Irene grew older, she and her friends would often perform plays in the forest on a wooden "stage" that was built for them. One day, when she was fifteen years old, Irene and her father were on their way up to Vermont when he stopped the car, relocated to the back seat, and proceeded to read the newspaper. He then asked Irene to get behind the wheel and start driving the vehicle. Evidently, in her father's eyes, the best way to learn was through experience and diligent practice. Irene credits her driving abilities, to this day, to the teachings of her dad when young. Irene believes her father, in many ways, had an immense influence on who she is today. She admired his dominating personality. even stating, "The final decision was always his." Irene also shared a close relationship with her mother, Bess, stating that she was an exceptional, caring, and bright lady. Although her mother never worked while the children were growing up, Irene smiles when thinking about her mother later in life taking on a job at Jordan Marsh during the holiday season. Bess loved working there.

Irene's family identified as Jewish, which her father observed by attending High Holiday services and her mother by lighting Shabbat candles every Friday night. She recalls her grandparents often speaking to her in their native tongue of Yiddish, allowing her to learn a few words every so often. Even so, Irene did not feel genuinely connected to Jewish customs, and in fact, it never took prominence in her life. She took a liking to learn about new religions, often attending church services with her housekeepers or friends when young to gain a diverse understanding of ethnicities.

Irene recalls meeting her husband, Norman, at the age of seventeen due to some facilitation on her mother's friend's part. Her mom, Bess, was an active member of Hadassah; during one of the meetings, Bess met the mother of Norman. Collectively, the two moms decided that their children should meet. Thus, after that encounter, Norman reached out to Irene, asking if she would like to accompany him on a date. Because of his friendly nature while speaking to her, Irene accepted the offer. The first date came and went, and then another, and from that point forward their relationship perpetuated. When they met, Norman was in the Navy, taking mandatory courses at Tufts School of Engineering. When he was sent to the Pacific to serve for about a year, the couple's romance survived through letter correspondence alone. Upon his return, within a few weeks, Irene and Norman got engaged. They soon made their relationship official through marriage in 1947, when Irene was nineteen and Norman was twenty-two. In 1950, Irene and Norman had their first child, Steven, and soon after, in 1952, their daughter Joan came along.

On June 6th, 1944, Irene graduated from high school on the momentous D-Day and opted to take a gap year to work with her father as a lab technician. After that, Irene began her undergraduate studies at the University of Rhode Island. One day, after Norman had returned from service and was residing in Boston, Irene distinctly recalls one of her friends rushing into her dorm room with the news of her acceptance to Boston University School of Education. Her friend relayed how easy the process was, stating that the application did not require any work. Emboldened by the words of her peer, Irene decided she wanted to switch universities. Irene hopped onto the next train from Providence to Boston. Upon arriving, she headed over to Boston

University's School of Education and successfully enrolled as an undergraduate student majoring in education.

When Irene got married, she had completed two years of undergraduate school but decided to take a break. About ten years later, she returned to school and earned her bachelor's degree from Boston University School of Education. Once her children grew up and were self-sufficient, Irene enrolled at Antioch College, which offered courses at Harvard at the time, and obtained her Master of Education.

Irene initiated her teaching career as a substitute. However, a school principal soon talked her into taking a full-time position. While she never planned on being a teacher in the first place, nor was she considering having a classroom of her own, she took the opportunity that came her way, merely to see what the result would be. At the end of her career, she looked back with a sense of accomplishment for what she had completed, finding a teacher role to be a very fulfilling position to take on. For twenty-five years, Irene taught second and fifth graders, with a preference for the latter, because she felt she could connect with the older kids to a greater degree. Living in Milton, MA, she pursued her teaching role within her town's public school system. At the time, all of the female teachers districtwide wore only dresses to work each day. However, one day, Irene diverged from this norm when she elected to wear slacks—the first teacher in Milton to have done so. Irene remembers that her clothing choice was the talk among students who would purposefully walk by her classroom to see her wearing slacks. It was unprecedented at the time.

After retiring from teaching at the age of sixty-five, Irene did not take it easy. Instead, as parents who wanted to help their kids, both Norman and Irene worked for their son, Steven, and his wife, Marilyn, at their travel agency in Boston. Every week, Irene and Norm would spend three days working; her duties included purchasing business supplies and collecting hotel commissions. Until the business was sold years later, the couple spent their time helping at the agency in any way possible. During this time, Norman and Irene decided to move into Orchard Cove, where Irene has now lived for over twenty-five years. Because she was one of the first residents to move into the "Cove" side of the property, the community considers her as one of the "Pioneers."

Even when she no longer worked with her son, Irene continued to help, but now for her daughter, Joan, who owns a decorative paint business. Before the COVID-19 health crisis made her unable to do so, at the age of ninety-one, Irene went to her daughter's art studio weekly to clean all paint cans, brushes, and buckets used from the workweek prior. Beyond that, Irene completed the meticulous work of writing down the names and numbers of paint colors and organizing, as well as listing, the paint cans in their proper order. The role was demanding, yet it was a pastime that Norman had helped his daughter with before his passing in 2003. Irene wanted to continue his work. While both mother and daughter worked simultaneously on different tasks during the day, they always took a lunch break together, which Irene cherished dearly.

Irene communicated how grateful she is to have her kids' presence in her life, as they always take good care of her and provide advice to guide decisions. Even so, at the age of ninety-two, Irene continues to maintain her independence by driving herself to most appointments, which she is thankful she can do, for she does not want to be a burden on her children. Her two grandsons and one great-granddaughter are the sunshine in her days, as she loves spending quality time with them. She considers her children and their progeny to be her greatest accomplishment in life, and she hopes they remember how much she cared for them and took an interest in their endeavors.

While living at Orchard Cove, Irene prioritizes keeping physically and mentally busy through a variety of activities, such as exercising, attending short story workshops, solving crossword puzzles, reading the newspaper to stay updated, and delving into whatever programs pique her interest.

Irene believes to have learned countless lessons from her own life experiences, but the most memorable ones she gained were from her husband. Norman would often say, "Who cares if your car gets dented? It is only a piece of tin." He always placed importance on his family's health and safety. Irene, too, learned to put family over everything and to overlook the smaller, immaterial things in life.

Irene also understands the significance of being tolerant and accepting toward others who are different. Her husband emanated tolerance in daily life by exuding so much care for people, regardless of their background. Irene prides herself in adopting this same philosophy. Irene feels that honesty—both to herself and her loved ones—is paramount to leading a fulfilling life. Beyond that, she believes in the importance of respect, education, and of course, love.

XI. Iris

To this day, walking into a hardware store brings back a flood of nostalgia from Iris' childhood. When young, she often visited the auto and hardware supply store that her uncle founded, "Benny's," which later developed into an extensive chain. While the store primarily sold car parts and tools, it also carried toys for the young ones. Every Christmas, Iris looked forward to stopping by the store, for she was given the liberty to pick out anything she wanted. On one occasion, she recalls choosing a doll, which she subsequently named Dale, and an accompanying carriage. Benny's is where Iris' father, Manuel, worked daily as a buyer and advertiser.

Iris always looked up to her father, noting him as one of the most influential people in her life. She admires the values he had always adhered to, and believes that her morals and own values developed from observing her father's actions. She cherishes the memories from the moments she spent with him when young, especially their daily drives in the summertime from their vacation spot in Narragansett to Benny's in Providence.

Iris, born in 1937, grew up in the suburbs of Providence, RI, even though the downtown city area was where she truly loved spending her time due to the lively crowd and constant excitement. Her secondary school career was entirely spent in Providence, where Iris attended Hope High School until her graduation in 1955.

Iris reminisces on her rich experiences as a young girl, and she firmly believes that her childhood years shaped who she is today. Her time was often spent socializing with her clique of friends, playing with dolls, or enjoying days at the beach. Her love for the ocean stems from experiences she had as a little girl, as she would often spend her summers on Narragansett Pier sitting under the boardwalk and playing Hilo Jack with her peers. In the winter time, she found pleasure in sledding down the hill near her home.

Beyond that, Iris treasured family gatherings, which is how her loved ones celebrated annual Jewish holidays. Passover was her favorite, for her entire family would share a meal. When young, her family would often attend temple, and Iris would go to weekly Sunday School classes. Iris feels as if her Jewish heritage is a very noteworthy aspect of her life, for the lessons she learned in Jewish teachings solidified her moral integrity.

Iris, her parents, and her sister Paula often took day trips together, and sometimes longer car trips to Florida. There, they visited Bubby Zlata, her father's mother, or Mama Mary, her maternal grandma, both who played integral roles in her life. Iris recalls the vibrant, art-deco buildings of Miami Beach, where her grandmothers resided, and eating lunch at Woolfie's Jewish style deli. When young, Iris remembers an underlying sisterly rivalry between her and her five-year younger sibling, Paula. Iris felt as if she had lost much of her parents' attention once her sister was born, causing some strain between the two. Over the years, however, the relationship between her and her sister strengthened. As adults, they speak to each other daily.

As a teenager, Iris' parents were very protective of her. She never provoked trouble and maintain excellent behavior. Adhering to her parents' expectations was important to her. Iris desired to excel in the school environment while still maintaining a social life. She enjoyed interacting with her friends and often spent free time going to The Liberty Theatre and on dates. Junior and senior prom were two nights she will never forget, for dressing up in a prom dress was so special.

After successfully completing high school, Iris exchanged one city for another when she embarked on two years of study at Boston University, majoring in public relations and communications. She chose this area of focus because of her aptitude to connect with people and learn more about the histories of individuals. After receiving her associate's degree at Boston University, Iris married her first husband, Ron, at the age of twenty. The couple initially moved to a home in Randolph. Iris' primary focus was her responsibility as a mother to her three children: Vicki, Heidi, and Mitchell. Her son, Mitchell, was named after Iris' father, Manuel, who died suddenly from cardiac arrest. This was a way to honor his legacy, as well as to respect the Jewish customs of baby naming.

As a mother, she ensured all three of her children gained exposure to Jewish customs by becoming members of a temple. She was also very active within her children's academic community, for she served as the President of the Parent Teacher's Association and actively involved herself in the Creative Arts Committee. She socialized with other parents, especially her best friend Sandy, who sadly lost her life at the age of forty due to Hodgkin's Disease. Looking back, Iris fondly thinks of Sandy as someone who greatly influenced her as a result of their cherished friendship.

After deciding to part ways with her first husband in her early forties, Iris began attending lectures and learning sessions on divorce and separation in Cambridge, MA. One meeting, she remembers with distinctness. After listening to a lawyer deliver a speech to the audience, Iris entered an elevator to leave the building. There, Iris met Bill—her future husband and the love of her life. After a few moments of conversing, Bill asked Iris if she would like to go out for a cup of coffee. Upon doing so, Bill then offered to pick Iris up from her home in Newton to attend the next meeting in the series together. This encounter was the beginning of the couple's loving relationship. After three years of dating, Iris and Bill officially married in 1988 and shared a beautiful wedding celebration at the Wellesley Inn that she planned entirely. With their union, both Iris and Bill became stepparents, and for Iris in particular, the stepmother of two lovely women—Suzy and Michelle.

Beyond her marriage and children, Iris noted that earning a master's degree was one of her greatest achievements. While in her mid-forties, Iris desired to return to school and fulfill a goal that she had long anticipated. As she had only received her associate's degree prior, she decided to attend Northeastern University, where she successfully earned her Bachelor of Arts in Sociology degree. Later, with the support of Bill, Iris obtained her Master of Social Work degree at Boston College. As part of the curriculum, Iris took on two internships, one of which took place at the Rogerson House, a retirement community. She treasured the connections she created with the residents. With a passion for interacting with others, she knew that a career in social work would be fulfilling.

Iris found her place as a geriatric social worker in a multitude of nursing homes, stating that was the population she gravitated toward. Additionally, she spent four years working at VNA Hospice, where she had the unique opportunity to counsel patients and work with families. She cherished her job and found great fulfillment within her twenty-year career.

Iris and Bill lived in Needham for about thirty years until they transitioned to Orchard Cove in 2017. Iris was a weekly attendee of Friday night services at the chapel, finding them peaceful and meditative. Although Bill was born into an Irish Catholic family, he always demonstrated flexibility and comfort with living in a predominantly Jewish community. He even engaged in certain Jewish customs, such as lighting candles or attending Pesach seders, out of love for his wife. Bill, a light in Iris' life, was known in the community for his talent in playing the guitar and his kind spirit, demonstrated by his efforts to help cats in need of care. Iris has always been an avid reader and learner, and also prides herself in serving as a buddy to other residents. Beyond that, she is a movie-buff, even serving on the movie committee. She's found so much joy in exploring other ethnicities and cultures, finding that it adds richness to her perspective on life. The couple was also the proud parents of their frisky, orange cat "Pumpkin."

On May 24th, 2019, Iris lost one of the most important people in her life, when her husband, Bill, suddenly passed away from cardiac arrest. Losing him left a distinguishable void in her life, serving as a source of daily sadness. Yet, despite this, Iris ensures that his memory lives on in many ways, including his love for folk music, family, and his adventurous personality. The couple shared a deep passion for music, and liked listening to their wedding song, "What I Did for Love" by Josh Groban. Iris often calls upon "Alexa" to play an array of her favorite melodies, including Irish music, Frank Sinatra, Sondheim, and show tunes. Iris has also been an active performer in the chorus, as well a singer in musicals, both which serve as means to stay connected to the musical art form.

Iris described Bill's "book of projects," or a comprehensive list of things he had hoped to do someday. In his remembrance, Iris decided to create a journal of her own. Within her list, she included many small goals, such as acting in a play, buying something outlandish, challenging her brain, learning new skills, and going on a ride with no destination. One thing that she does not foresee herself doing is flying somewhere to attend a baseball game and then returning home, all within one day. That was an endeavor Bill successfully took on only a few months before his passing. His dream was to travel to stadiums nationwide.

After his passing, Iris made it her mission to be only kind and compassionate to others, as that is what Bill embodied in his everyday life. From her relationship with Bill, Iris undeniably understood the true meaning of love. As expressed in Iris' words, "Love is when you think of someone else first." Iris concluded that a "good marriage reflects in knowing that someone else unconditionally loves you and will be there for your children." That is exactly how Iris described her thirty-one-year marriage with Bill.

The most important thing to Iris, at the age of eighty-three years old, is to be a good parent and nana to her five children and seven grandchildren. Family matters most, and she makes sure to communicate with her kids every night on the phone. She hopes to keep her mind sharp and continue listening to others with open thoughts and undivided attention. While some may think becoming a grandmother is a sign of losing youth, according to Iris, she feels as if it is an incredible role to play. As a grandmother, she can reap the rewards, without possessing the responsibilities of parenthood. Iris has always maintained a strong family identity, a quality which she hopes to have passed onto her kids.

Iris believes she's lived life, thus far, using her values of integrity, honesty, and compassion—qualities that she channels from her father who exemplified them. Like everything in life,

Iris' values have evolved over the years. With that said, one thing she hopes has remained constant over time is her kindness.

Iris is forever thankful for the influence of her aunt and uncle, Eve and Sam, who acted as second parents when she was a child. She felt loved unconditionally by this couple and gained immense insight from them on how to act with kindness.

Iris looks back upon her life as if it were a three-act play: starting with her childhood and teenage years, then her first marriage with Ron and the birth of her three children, and lastly, her marriage with Bill, her husband who motivated her to go to graduate school and become a certified social worker. At the age of eighty-three years, Iris believes to be living in the final, yet lengthy, scene of the third act. While all three acts have had their moments of happiness and sorrow, she feels fulfilled for what she has achieved. When asked how she hopes to be remembered, she said by her "spirit, compassion, sense of humor, and love of life." Beyond that, she hopes her family recalls that sometimes, just sometimes, she acted slightly improper. As Iris said, "It was just in my genes!"

XII. Ina

On Thanksgiving Day 1932, Ina's mother certainly had a lot to be thankful for. Her first, and only, child was born. Anecdotally, Ina learned that the hospital delivered her mother a turkey meal, with all the fixings, to her room for dinner. Undoubtedly, that was a Thanksgiving feast her mother would never forget. As Ina grew older, she cherished that her birthday often fell around or on the Thanksgiving holiday. It allowed her the opportunity to celebrate her special day with those she loved the most.

As an only child, Ina felt showered with love. For the first six years of her life, she resided in a two-story, one-bathroom home in Chelsea, MA, alongside her parents, maternal grandparents, and two aunts. The attic of the house was rented out and occupied by two boarders. Their abode might have been filled, yet it never felt crowded. Her grandfather, a shoe cobbler, conducted business from the back porch of the home, making it so customers would come and go when need be. It was a pleasant

119

place for Ina to spend her formative years, and it was especially enjoyable because she was always the center of attention.

The Chelsea home was the central location for family events. Her grandparents had seven children, and most of them were married and had children of their own. The family was extensive, making holiday gatherings incredibly lively and hectic. Passover was a celebration that stood foremost in Ina's mind, for all would assemble around the table and listen intently to her grandfather lead the seder. Ina chuckled upon remembering her mother advising her which gefilte fish to eat and which not to eat, for the one prepared by one of the aunts was always repulsive. As a child, Ina possessed the aspiration to learn Hebrew and to become Bat Mitzvah. Her family was Orthodox, yet her parents became members of a local conservative synagogue to allow her to take Hebrew school courses. Ina soon realized that she was much older than all the other children in her class, making her uncomfortable to continue. So, she left. She never became a Bat Mitzvah. Nonetheless, Judaism remained a critical aspect of her life. She not only appreciated her own heritage, but she found it essential to learn about other cultures as well. To pursue this desire, in college, she took courses on comparative religion, finding it fascinating to gain knowledge on Christianity and Islam. In Ina's perspective, understanding others' identities is integral to being a well-rounded, educated citizen. One of the values she has held closest to her is always being tolerant and respectful of others.

As a young girl, Ina fell in love with the pastime of reading—a passion that has persisted her entire lifetime. This fondness for literature could likely be attributed to one of the aunts whom Ina lived with, an individual she referred to as her second mother. Her aunt often brought home books for her to peruse, and the best part was there was always such great variety in her selections. Whether it was a children's edition of a Shakespearean play, a classic Grimm's fairytale, or a book filled with poems for Ina to memorize, she found happiness in reading it. Her lifelong desire to read rooted from her Aunt Freda, and for that, she was grateful.

Amid the Great Depression, Ina's father purchased a small bakery shop a few streets away from her grandparents' home. He worked diligently to maintain a successful business, and he ensured quality goods by mixing all the dough by hand. Ina distinctly recalls her father slaving over the big tub of dough, continuously stirring until it was ready to be put in the coal oven. Above the store, one could find a small apartment composed of a kitchen and one large bedroom. After six years living with her grandparents and aunts, Ina and her parents moved into their own cozy residence above the bakery. She slept in the same room as her parents, for that is all that the space allowed. From this, Ina learned a vital value—make the best of what you have and do not long for something more. During one particular year, the family allowed an extra guest to stay in their room as well. The guest was her cousin, Herb, who was spending a year in Boston's Naval Yard before entering the United States Air Force. He took on the night shifts, allowing Ina to sleep in her bed during the nighttime and Herb to sleep in it during the day. Despite the small size of the apartment, family was essential to Ina and her parents. It was in their nature to allow a loved one to stay if need be. In the apartment, summertime was intolerably hot, but thankfully, Ina's aunt lived in Maine and often brought her niece up there to escape the heat. It was a peaceful getaway, yet it also allowed Ina to spend time with her four cousins that lived there. Ina did not have siblings, so the close bond she shared with her cousins was special to her.

Living amid World War II changed the way Americans conducted their lives and consumed material goods. Ina especially remembers the usage of stamps and the strict rationing of butter and sugar. Yet, despite the challenges that accompanied this era, Ina always did her part to help the cause. Metal was essential for the war efforts, as it allowed for the construction of vehicles, weaponry, and other equipment. Ina and her friends would often scour the streets for metal items, such as tin foil gum wrappers and tin cans, to contribute to the collection. Once the search was complete, they brought the wagon full of scraps to a collection center where it would later be boiled down to a usable form.

In 1944, after six years of living in the apartment above the bakery, Ina's parents purchased a small home only a couple of streets over from her father's shop. The bottom floor was rented out, yet the top floor provided them a cozy kitchen, living room, and two bedrooms. It was the perfect size for Ina and her parents. At the time of the move, she was twelve and attending middle school. From kindergarten to high school graduation, Ina always adored going to school, and unlike other children at the time, she never resented the required work out of the classroom. Learning brought excitement and enrichment to her life. Despite the negative stereotypes often attached to the high school experience, Ina found hers to be nothing but pleasant. She was highly immersed in activities, such as becoming the yearbook editor, and created close friendships with her peers. Because of her love for literature, her favorite subject was always English. Yet, she excelled in all areas and achieved high grades. In fact, Ina was titled valedictorian of her high school class.

Ina was the daughter of two immigrants, her mother from Lithuania and her father from Poland. Her dad had traveled to the United States when he was eighteen years of age, bringing along his two younger siblings. It was not in the plans for him to make the trip alone, but his mother had tragically passed away amid the arduous journey to obtain the family's visas. Both Ina's father and mother had received little formal education, for they both spent their time working when they moved to the United States. When Ina was in high school, there was a sentiment that children born from immigrant parents were perhaps less intelligent and incapable of reaching high success. Once, a teacher announced to a group of students, "You all know Ina does so well. If she were to come from immigrant parents, she would not have done so well." Ironically, this was not the case. Ina was upset by the statement, for not only was it untruthful, but she was proud to be the daughter of two immigrants. Ina felt as if her mother especially had a positive influence on her. Her mom was accepting of every challenge that came her way and dealt with adversity with poise. Because of her mother, Ina shared that same outlook on overcoming obstacles.

Ina remembers her high school graduation day distinctly, and not for reasons one might expect. This day was the only time Ina's mother, Fannie, ever raised her voice to her husband. Both parents were exceptionally proud of their daughter. Yet, their philosophies on whether or not Ina should attend college diverged. Her father continuously said it was not a necessary use of time or money, as it was likely that Ina would merely grow up to be a wife and mother. Her college education would not benefit her when changing diapers. During her senior year of high school, Ina secured a job at a local dentist's office to learn how to take X-rays and make filling mixtures. Her father assumed that she could continue in this role if she genuinely wanted to work. He could not wrap his head around her desire to secure her degree. Fannie, however, thought her husband was acting foolish. Even though her mother had not received a college education, she wanted to ensure her daughter, Ina, had the opportunity to continue learning and find success for herself.

When it came down to choosing which college to attend, the choice was clear for Ina. She knew she wanted to study at the University of Massachusetts Amherst (UMass Amherst). Not only did her boyfriend attend the school, but it was affordable and allowed her the authentic on-campus college experience that she had strongly desired. With that said, her choice of college was not met by enthusiasm from all. Before graduation day, her principal called her into his office and asked her to reconsider her university choice. The prior valedictorians had always attended Mount Holyoke, Radcliffe, or one of the other prestigious Ivy League universities.

Like many things throughout her life, Ina was adamant about her choice. Beyond strong academics and the experience of living on campus, UMass Amherst had awarded her a scholarship due to her impressive performance in high school. She stood her ground, stating UMass Amherst was the right college for her. No one could change her mind.

125

For her first two years at UMass Amherst, Ina spent time with her boyfriend, and later husband, Aaron. The two met at the end of Ina's junior year of high school, at a friend's graduation party. Aaron had also attended Chelsea High School, but when they first met, he had just completed his freshman year at UMass Amherst. The couple began dating that summer.

In Ina's home, her mother replaced the piano in the living room with a television set. In line with her characteristic loving and thoughtful personality, Fannie wanted to make sure the two kids had television to pass the time together. Both of Ina's parents took a liking to Aaron immediately and were accepting of their relationship. From that point onward, their relationship flourished. By the time Ina's sophomore year of college came to a close, Aaron had just graduated and was now venturing off to the University of Maryland to secure his Ph.D. At this point, the couple knew they were going to get married. Yet, Ina also knew that, since her husband was going to graduate school, she had to support the couple financially once she received her degree. So, for her, this meant a change of plans.

At this time, there was a demand for teachers in the area of elementary education. So, to ensure a job post-graduation, Ina desired to switch her major to this field. The problem was, UMass did not offer a major in elementary education, yet Boston University (BU) did. Thus, Ina transferred to BU for the last four semesters of college and secured her Bachelor of Science in Elementary Education soon after. She continued her studies during the summer, which allowed her to graduate early. Because BU's campus was so close to her family's Chelsea home, it was far more cost-effective for Ina to commute. Even so, it was a bit of a hassle to do so. To get to class every day, she had to take the bus, then a subway, and finally a streetcar. While in school, Ina taught at the Devotion School in Brookline. Her commute also heavily relied on the usage of public transportation.

Ina and Aaron were married soon after she graduated from BU, and from there, the couple both lived in a small apartment in Maryland. At the age of twenty-one, Ina began teaching a forty-student class, on her own, at an elementary school situated within a low-income community. Ina loved teaching, as well as her interaction with the young students. Ironically enough, her maiden name, "Melamed" means teacher in Hebrew. Her last name was certainly fitting for the career she chose to pursue.

During her first year teaching, there was one student whom Ina developed a particular fondness for. His name was George; he was nine years old at the time and unbelievably sweet. For the majority of Ina's students, facing hardship at home was not uncommon. For George, his mother was a single parent to three children, and as Ina soon discovered, it was difficult for her to care for her children financially. As a result, Ina often paid a quarter or so for George to go on class field trips because she knew that he would not have the opportunity to go otherwise. On Halloween day, all forty students went home for lunch, which they did every day, and they were asked to return dressed in a costume for the school's annual Halloween parade. However, when the bell signaling the end of lunch rang, only thirty-nine kids were present in the classroom. George was not there. When the school day had closed, Ina walked over to George's family's apartment and knocked on the door. The door swung open, and there he was, staring back at her. Ina asked, "George, why did you not return to school?" He looked at her, replying, "I did not have a costume." She replied, "You should have told me. I would have gotten you one."

A few months later, Ina was called down to the office of the school principal. In their meeting, she explained that George's mother had called the school, asking if Ina would like to adopt her son. His mom could not handle three kids any longer, and she knew that Ina cared for him. Now, this request indeed came as a shock to Ina. At the time, she had just entered her twenties, and George was nine years old. For a bit of time, she considered the offer. Without a doubt, she wanted to help as much as she could. Yet, she was not in the proper place to take on that responsibility. Aaron and Ina lived in a two-room apartment, leaving no room for a young boy to live. Although she declined the offer, she continued to care for George's wellbeing while teaching.

Throughout the years, Ina always wondered what had happened to young George and where life took him.

After three years of teaching in Maryland, the couple relocated to a new home in the small town of Albion, NY. Aaron took on a new job at Bird's Eye, working as a food technologist in their research lab. Upon moving to this area, Ina and Aaron knew they wanted to begin their family together. Thus, rather than taking on a full-time teaching commitment, Ina began to substitute teach. Ina became pregnant for the first time while in Albion, yet in her seventh month, Aaron secured a job position in the Washington, D.C. area. They moved to a home in Maryland, and her son Seth was born there. Only two years after the first, the couple's daughter, Susan, came along. While her kids were young, stay at home mothering became her full-time priority. The children's toddler years were spent in Maryland, but when Susan turned four, the family moved to a new place: Sharon, MA.

Ina's cousin always raved about how nice the Sharon area was. They soon discovered this to be true for themselves. Beyond that, the location made for an easy commute for Aaron, who now worked at Stop and Shop food laboratories. When the children got older, Ina returned to what she loved to do—teaching. She instructed at the Solomon Schechter School in Newton for many years. In her late forties, Ina changed positions to Children's Director at the local Jewish Community Center (JCC).

Meanwhile, during this time, her son, Seth, had attended Brandeis University for his undergraduate studies. There, he met his future wife, and in 1980, the couple got married. However, only three months after the wedding, tragedy struck the family. Aaron, Ina's first love, passed away suddenly from a heart attack at the young age of fifty-one years. At the time, Ina had just begun her role at the JCC. However, when news spread that her husband passed away, she received support from the parents of students and her colleagues at Schechter. Parents of past students crafted kind notes, not only extending their condolences but explaining the influence Ina had on the lives of their children. During the difficult times she was enduring, reading the notes was both uplifting and gratifying. One of the messages Ina had received was from the mother of John, a young boy who was exceptional in writing. His mom thanked Ina for complimenting and guiding his writing skills development. Low and behold, John became a professional Hollywood screenwriter when he grew up.

While grieving the loss of her first husband, Ina returned to the JCC to resume her responsibilities. She found joy in planning afterschool and vacation activities for the children. Often, during school vacation, JCC staff would bring the children on field trips to various sites. Once, the field trip of choice was to the Boston Children's Theatre to watch the Peter Pan production. However, on their journey to the playhouse, the school bus broke down on the Southeast Expressway heading to the city. This situation posed an issue, as there was a busload of eager children who were not going to sit patiently while the replacement bus was on the way. Ina quickly determined a solution. As the children brought packed lunches, and because she had a copy of the Peter Pan book with her, Ina spent time reading the story while the kids ate. This resulted in a positive effect, for the children were now knowledgeable of the play plot before seeing the performance. After years in the Children's Director position, Ina switched roles to become the Senior Adult Director at the JCC. She diligently worked to create meaningful events for the elderly population, and she spearheaded the senior adult program at the Stoughton, MA JCC. Having gone to Israel four times, Ina felt as if she had the opportunity to immerse herself into the culture. Yet, among the four times, there was one particular trip that remains prominent in Ina's mind. On a trip with eleven of her fellow staff members from the JCC, she adventured across Israel on a private bus with a tour guide. Since she was the Senior Adult Director at the time, Ina had the exciting experience of going to Lifeline for the Elderly, a senior citizen center in Jerusalem. She learned about all the beautiful things that were done for Israel's senior community to feel like productive citizens despite their age.

After seventeen years of work at the JCC, Ina retired. She found a great deal of satisfaction from her positions as program directors and as a teacher. That said, there was always a part of her that wondered if she could have done more. As an individual who loved to learn about the world around her, she felt as if there was more to pursue and acquire knowledge about. Nonetheless, she was satisfied.

Eight years after she lost her first husband, Ina married a second time to a man named Hillel. He was a caring and kind individual who was part of a large family that treated Ina with respect and love. Hillel was observant of Orthodox Judaism, and soon Ina also assumed an Orthodox lifestyle. Hillel had fled Germany during the Holocaust, along with his family. Later in life, he had hoped to return to Germany to witness whatever remained from that period. The German government extended invitations to people who had fled from the country when young to venture on an unabridged tour of Berlin, all the while witnessing the remnants from the Holocaust. In the late 1990s, Hillel accepted this invite, and the couple traveled to Berlin together. For fourteen days, Ina and Hillel traveled around with a bus chock full of people. The tour left nothing unhidden, admitting to the atrocities brought on by the Nazi regime. Tours were given solely in German, yet Hillel retained his memory of the language and thus could translate for Ina. Besides, Ina was strong in Yiddish, and the two languages resembled each other. It was an eye-opening and painful experience, yet in each other's company, they had a lovely time.

Sadly, after fifteen short years of marriage, Hillel passed away. Even so, his family has stayed in close contact with Ina as she is still part of their lives. Following fifty years of living in her Sharon residence, in 2018, Ina moved to a senior living community, Orchard Cove.

At the age of eighty-seven, the most crucial thing to Ina is her family's happiness and safety. As a parent, she has cherished the opportunity to watch her son and daughter grow and develop to become contributing members of society. After going to Brandeis, Seth became an executive director at a prestigious university in Boston. Following her undergraduate studies at Brown University and Boston University Law School, her daughter, Susan, now works in government affairs for pharmaceutical companies. Ina is proud of all they have accomplished, for their hard work and positive attitudes have paid off. Parenting was nothing but a joyful experience, despite being tiring at times. For Ina, becoming a grandparent was an entirely different story. She felt as if her four grandchildren were a luxury; they are people in her life to love and enjoy. She hopes they never forget how much she loves them and wishes nothing but good health for them always.

Upon being asked what her most significant accomplishment was in life, Ina replied that it was her ability to make the best of every situation. She has faced an exorbitant amount of hardship, and at eighty-seven, she continues to do so fighting a battle with a serious illness. Yet, just like everything that came her way, Ina continues to persevere. She hopes to promote the message for others to do the same.

XIII. Charles "Bud"

In 1932, Bud became the seventh, and last, member of his immediate family. The five children and their parents, Sadie and Philip, lived in a small home in Stoughton, MA, where Bud recalled little to no privacy. That could be contributed to the fact that he shared a room with his older sister until she was eighteen. When young, Bud enjoyed coasting, skating, and board games, like Monopoly. His siblings used the family's one bike and one snow sled; thus, sharing became an important aspect of his childhood.

His family observed all of the primary Jewish holidays and attended synagogue on Yom Kippur, yet Passover festivities were the most prominent within his household. For first and second grade, Bud went to a one-room schoolhouse with a single outhouse, located just down the road from his home. He later attended Stoughton public schools until his graduation in 1950.

135

While he reminisces on his childhood with fond memories, he also pointed out that money did not come easy for his family, forcing his father to find work through multiple avenues. He remembers his parents as two loving individuals who provided for him and his siblings to the best of their financial ability. They always ensured that the children's needs of food and healthcare were met. As a child, he never had a superfluous number of possessions, yet he was thankful for what he had. He credits his upbringing to his current desire to give back, for later in life, he had the means to share with others.

At a young age, Bud learned to be very conscious of his decisions, especially those dealing with money, and he believed that this attitude guided his decisions in adulthood. With an understanding of his family's economic situation, Bud never asked for money, but instead developed an industrious spirit to provide for himself. Thus, he worked in a myriad of places, including grocery stores, chicken and cattle farms, and a local factory that made heels and rubber for shoes. Bud says he "has never been one to wish for things, but he works for them."

Later, Bud enrolled in Northeastern University in Boston, majoring in marketing and advertising. Under Northeastern's co-op plan, Bud found a job as an office boy at the Boston Traveler, an afternoon newspaper. He later took on a role at the Boston Herald for a short period, working as a full-time sports copy editor. During his college years, Bud met his future wife, Roz, upon being introduced by a shared acquaintance.

Like many other American families at the time, WWII took a tremendous toll on Bud and his loved ones. With all three of his brothers serving in the military, Bud recalls the three-star flag draped in the front window of his childhood home, symbolizing their contribution to the efforts. His brother, Herb, was drafted into the U.S. Army, and another brother, Robert, served with the Navy Seabees.

Less than a year after graduating from college, in 1956, Bud was drafted into the military for two years. In March of 1956, he began his basic training at Fort Dix, NJ, where he was a squad leader. After completing this program three months later, he headed off to Fort Gordon in Augusta, GA. Within the Army, due to his background as an editor, Bud was assigned to the role of battalion clerk, with duties including the upkeep of records, typing, and drafting of letters. Bud recalls his time in Georgia to be eye-opening, for it was the first time he gained exposure to a racist culture with prejudice against Black people. The "White Only" signs posted on doorways of bathrooms or at water fountains shocked him, as such segregation was not prevalent in the north.

On Christmas Day, 1956, Bud and Roz got married in Brighton, MA. Their honeymoon was the drive south to Augusta, where they happily resided in an efficiency apartment. While in Georgia, Roz and Bud had their first daughter, Sherri, in 1958. Upon discharge from service that same year, the growing family relocated to Brighton, where their second daughter, Lisa, was born. They soon felt as if they had outgrown the size of the apartment, and with the possibility of expanding the family further, they knew it was time to move to the suburbs. They bought a home in Randolph, MA, which had a large and growing Jewish community. It was a small, yet adequate, residence and here, their third and final daughter, Barbara, was born.

Upon returning from the service, Bud continued working where he left off at the Boston Herald, serving as a sports copy and layout editor. However, in 1967, he was laid off from his job due to the Boston Herald and Boston Traveler merging into one company. Feeling panicked and anxious, Bud needed to secure a new job rapidly to support his family. Thankfully, after two weeks, Bud was hired as a sports copy editor by the Boston Globe, and later, he became a picture editor who oversaw photograph choice as well as the writing of captions. Within his role, Bud often would mentor young reporters and provide them with advice to reach success. Climbing up the ladder, Bud soon was promoted to Assistant Night News Editor, and later Night News Editor, where he oversaw the nighttime news operation. He played an integral role in designing pages and often made choices on what to display on the front page of the Boston Globe, which thousands of Bostonians would read the following morning.

Then, in 1978, Bud forever changed the game. It was the year he introduced computers to the Globe newsroom, which soon took the place of typewriters completely and saved the company millions of dollars. Working with the system vendor, Atex, Bud helped design an efficient and sustainable computer system specifically catered to the Boston Globe's purposes. Alongside the vendor company, Bud worked diligently to streamline the system, create a user manual for all employees, and oversee all staff training. Due to his efforts, Bud was rewarded with the title of Director of Newsroom Technology. Because the system was received so well by the staff, Bud truly felt euphoric.

Once the system was well established, representatives from other newspapers would visit the Globe to witness the system in use. Throughout his time working for the Globe, Bud hosted hundreds of United States and world newsmen. Among them, he had guests from the Jerusalem Post, who bought the system.

After the Post decided to purchase and install it within their operation, Bud was invited to go to Israel and introduce the usage of the Atex system to all of their employees, who were, at first, a bit hesitant to adopt this new technology. Beyond that, he became president of the Atex Users Group, with his role encompassing many duties such as arranging a program for the annual conference, at the Kennedy Library in Boston, as well as making improvements and sharing information regarding the system. On one occasion, Bud served as the guest speaker at a European newspaper symposium in Holland, where he discussed the effectiveness of the system to the attendees.

Bud was a take-charge person, admitting that sometimes he had difficulty delegating tasks. With such passion for his work, he understandably wanted to ensure that his endeavors led to a successful outcome. In 1991, after a highly satisfying career at the Boston Globe, Bud accepted an early retirement package, at the age of fifty-nine. The same year, as all of their children were well into their pursuit of graduate degrees, Roz and Bud decided to move out of their Randolph home to live in a beautiful condo community in Foxboro. Despite retiring, Bud had difficulty with the thought of straying away from the business altogether, so he secured a part-time copy editor position at the Quincy Patriot Ledger. Because of the flexibility of this opportunity, after many years of diligent work, Bud and Roz had a chance to enjoy international travel to some degree.

During a conversation with Bud discussing his family life and career, he said, "I am the luckiest man I know," for all he has experienced. He is proud to be the "Mr. Fix It" in the family, always willing to repair what was broken and be a parent that is always present for his children when they needed help. He served as a living testament for why it is essential to find your passions and pursue them. While discussing his career in hindsight, he said, "I was on cloud nine. I was high on life, and I do not think I ever came down from it."

Bud reminisces on the unforgettable vacations he embarked on, including a cruise that stopped in St. Petersburg, Russia, where he attended shul for Shabbat services. Beyond that, as an avid bicycle rider, he enjoyed numerous Elderhostel biking trips in Europe. He remembered his two visits to beautiful Holland, biking on the Danube River's bike paths and stopping for overnight stays in small towns.

Bud was a fanatic for talk show programs and always stayed up to date on current events through his daily newspaper reading. Always one to reach out a helping hand, he spent his time during the COVID-19 pandemic calling others in the Orchard Cove community to ensure their wellbeing. Bud, an individual who valued a determined work ethic, believes his most significant accomplishment is persevering through a satisfying and rewarding job at the Boston Globe.

Bud is thrilled to reside in the Orchard Cove community, to be married to Roz, and to be the father of three successful children and the grandfather of four. Upon asking what he hopes to be remembered for 100 years from now, Bud wishes that the community recalls him as an individual who was kind to other people and who gave back to those who need it. Bud was fulfilled in the sense that he worked so hard in his lifetime, closing the interview by saying that his time with Roz at Orchard Cove were, "truly our golden years."

XIV. Roslyn "Roz"

As the youngest of three children and the only girl, Roz felt as if she was given special attention by her father, Moses. He absolutely adored her. She also had a strong relationship with her brother, Seymour, who was six years older and attended Clark University while living at home. A significant influence on her life, Seymour shared his passions with Roz by teaching her how to play football—particularly tackling—and bridge, among a variety of other things. Roz's other brother, Milton, was ten years older than her. He attended a university in Oklahoma for one year before being drafted in the U.S. Army during WWII. Roz recalls how Milton fought on the frontlines of the war, including in the Battle of the Bulge, as an infantry soldier with the 9th Army.

Born in 1934, Roz's young years were spent in her hometown of Worcester, MA, and they were a time of joyous memories. She often occupied her free time with reading, especially Nancy Drew novels, and also loved to play with her paper dolls.

Jewish heritage and values were an integral aspect of her childhood, and it continued to be that way as an adult. Along with other members of her social circle, Roz was heavily involved in the groups established by the local Jewish Community Center and Young Judea. Her father, considered to be a Talmudic scholar in Worcester, was a consistent attendee of weekly Shabbat services at their local synagogue. Her father was also a traveling male haberdashery salesman and an owner of his own business, known to his customers to have an honest reputation and to sell his products at a fair price. Roz considers her mother, Rebecca, to be "the best homemaker possible." Her mother was an avid knitter, often crafting gloves, hats, mittens, and some of her beautiful clothing. She also shares that her mother's "cooking and baking were the envy of many" in the community, and it often lured family members to the house for holiday dinners.

Roz cherishes some of her mother's knitted pieces to this day and continues to recreate some of the recipes her mom used when she was a child. Roz learned many vital lessons from her parents, but perhaps the most prominent of these teachings was how to live life ethically and morally. It was from them that she gained an understanding of how to know right from wrong.

After graduating valedictorian of her high school class, Roz began her college studies at Boston University with a major in elementary education. During Christmas break in 1953, Roz was invited to the home of one of her friends, a co-counselor at Camp Young Judea. Her friend also invited a young fellow named Bud. Several months later, Roz and Bud attended a Boston Pops Concert together, sitting in the front row—since Bud got free tickets—and listening to the melodies. As it is said, the rest is history. They were married in 1956. That same year, Bud was drafted into the United States Army and was stationed at Fort Gordon in Augusta, GA. The couple's honeymoon consisted of a road trip from Massachusetts to Georgia. At St. Joseph's hospital in Augusta, their first daughter, Sherri, was born.

When Sherri was two months old and knowing that Bud would soon be discharged from the Army, Roz and the baby flew to Worcester to stay in her parents' home for a brief period until Bud arrived. As Bud was making his way back north after being released from duty, he got stuck in the middle of a raging blizzard. With no cell phones at the time, there was no means to communicate with one another. A few days into the trip, Bud located a Howard Johnson's ice cream shop and called Roz, relieving her worries. Due to the weather, Bud arrived at her parents' home five days after departure for a trip that should have only taken two.

Soon after, Roz and Bud relocated to an apartment in Brighton. However, in 1960, after having their second child, Lisa, the family decided it was time to purchase their own residence in a suburban neighborhood. They bought a $12,000 home in Randolph because, at the time, the town had the largest Jewish population south of Boston. While living in this house, they had their third daughter, Barbara, or the family's "very own Barbie doll."

Roz and Bud ensured that their three daughters gained exposure to their Jewish background at a young age. Soon after moving into the town, the family became members of a local temple. Here, their three daughters attended Hebrew school, became Bat Mitzvah, and joined USY. Their daughter, Lisa, also worked as the secretary at the Hebrew school for several years.

Roz was always passionate about working with kids. When her children grew older, she decided it was time to re-initiate her teaching career. She approached the school board at the temple to ask if they would be interested in spearheading a pre-school program. After gaining approval, Roz began her twenty-one-year journey as director.

She oversaw a staff of twelve and was the head instructor for many of these young students. At the start, the program had ten students enrolled. However, as the school's reputation spread, and with much diligence, Roz was able to expand the program to include more than two hundred children with morning, afternoon, and all-day sessions.

Pertinent to the Massachusetts Office for Children's rules, it was required that students of all religious and ethnic backgrounds were able to enroll. However, with parents' knowledge, Roz ensured that the students celebrated every primary Jewish holiday and Shabbat in some form. She greatly enjoyed her interactions with the preschoolers, and in her words, she called her experience as pre-school director a labor of love. Today, these children's parents continue to express their gratitude to Roz for setting their kids on the right path.

In 1992, Roz and Bud moved to a beautiful condo community in Foxboro, where they resided for twenty-six years. By this time, their three daughters had earned college degrees. Their daughters are very successful, as two of them are lawyers, and one is a vice president of an international insurance company.

Upon moving to the residential community, Roz quickly became involved and was elected to the Board of Trustees and later to the chairperson. Alongside the other members, Roz oversaw the management company and worked to pass a rule that ensured that only three out of 106 condos in the community could be rented at any given time with approval by the Trustees. Roz was such an essential part of the board that, when the couple stated they were moving to a senior community, they presented her with a crystal star because they believed she was their shining star.

Later, the couple moved to a senior community. As the first residents in the community to move in, they cut the opening ribbon. In every community she enters, Roz immerses herself and interacts with her community members. This time was no different. Upon her arrival, Roz was asked to start the resident council and chair it as well. She also headed a holiday fundraiser, selling jewelry that she crafted herself.

However, Bud was not happy living within this community, as it was not the place he envisioned spending the remainder of his life. The couple searched for a new residence, and upon entering Orchard Cove for the first time, they knew this was the place for them. The welcoming, kind, and vibrant Jewish community drew them in from the start. Thus, Bud and Roz decided to move to Orchard Cove two weeks after their initial visit, in July 2018. At Orchard Cove, Bud serves as a member of the Hospitality Committee, a moderator of the current events programs, and a friend to so many. As a result of the COVID-19 health crisis, and Orchard Cove's response for temporary isolation, he took the initiative to call numerous residents to check on their wellbeing.

Roz is an avid mahjong and bridge player and has mentored applicants for the Orchard Cove Scholarship Committee. During the COVID-19 pandemic, Roz has gracefully adapted by finding ways to stay connected and occupied with her iPad. In Roz and

Bud's words, they are "both so thankful to be living at Orchard Cove."

At eighty-six years old, the most important thing to Roz is the health of her family and the welfare of her children and grandchildren. She genuinely cares about the state of this country, the direction of the political atmosphere, and ensuring a strong makeup of the Supreme Court. She recalls how fervid her father was about politics and how he would write letters to all the candidates. Like her father, Roz is passionate about the current and future political status of the United States. Roz and Bud are also both charter members of the Holocaust Museum in Washington, D.C.

She is a keen advocate for Israel's welfare, and she supports the nation to the best of her financial ability. She has traveled to Israel multiple times with Bud, including a trip when their daughter Barbara attended Hebrew University for a year.

Roz continues to embrace her Jewish heritage and lives by the values instilled within her. She enjoys celebrating the annual holidays, especially the Passover festivities. In the words of Roz herself, she has a "Jewish heart and soul."

XV. Richard "Dick"

Dick, born in 1927, was always proud to be a Bostonian, for he loved the ambiance of city life. Dick's parents, Samuel and Sarah, immigrated from Russia to the United States. During this transition, his father's original last name was forced to adapt to become more "Americanized." Dick was part of a large extended family, yet he was the youngest of all of his cousins. He recalls his childhood home to be the nucleus of all family activities and reminisces on Friday night Shabbat dinners, where his house was always crammed with relatives. As a child, the toys that occupied his time, such as carts, scooters, and roller skates, were often constructed with his own talents.

Looking back, Dick is reminded of a time when he played with a parachute and accidentally broke a neighbor's window. Although comedic in hindsight, it was not such a laughing matter at the time. Dick was grateful for all of his childhood family traditions and how there was such a great deal of care for one another. He recalls his mother staying at home for him and his sister, Cynthia, while his father often worked at his own store, which sold clothes to fishermen in Boston.

During the Second World War, economic hardship faced his family. Thus, in an effort to help out, Dick often spent time as a teenager assisting at his father's store. When he was young, Dick met his best friend, Stanley, while playing a game of ball. The two maintained a lifetime of friendship until Stanley's tragic passing at the young age of sixty-seven.

In 1945, at the age of seventeen years old and with the desire to serve his country, Dick decided to enroll in the Massachusetts Maritime Academy for a sixteen-month program. This opportunity would allow him to become a Naval officer at the finish. When he got out of the program, however, the war was over. During his training, Dick learned how to run an engineering room of a large ship and distill saltwater for drinking. After a short while going to sea in the merchant marines, in 1947, Dick ventured to Boston University (BU) to study business administration. When he was a junior, he was elected to Beta Gamma Sigma, a business honor society exclusive to academically high achieving students. At the time, Dick had his eyes set on becoming a football coach and believed a BU degree would put him on the right track. However, he later realized this was not the path for him. In 1950, after completing seven semesters, Dick graduated early from BU.

In 1949, Dick met his future-wife, Mae, when her cousin introduced them to one another. He recalls calling Mae to ask her if she would like to go on a movie dinner date. Their relationship bloomed from that point onward, developing so much so that they got married in 1951. Dick says marrying Mae was his most significant accomplishment in life.

During his time at BU, in 1948, Dick embarked on a new venture when he became a co-owner of a driving school and took part in teaching driving to students. By leveraging the business skills learned at school, Dick successfully expanded his business through partnerships with private academic institutions, where he taught their students how to drive. In 1954, Dick began his fulfilling career at Tremco, a construction product company, where he proceeded to spend the next thirty-five years working in management roles.

During our interview, Dick emphasized the importance of family in his life. Dick and Mae had four sons together—Gary, Glenn, Bradley, and Scott. The family suffered an immense loss when their son Scott tragically passed away at the young age of two and a half.

Upon asking Dick what the best thing about being a parent is, he replied "it is the opportunity to love and be loved," as well as to vicariously enjoy the successes of his children. He is ecstatic that his children care for one another, and he is appreciative to have observed their growth over the years. He is just so proud of them, and he hopes they always act ethically as human beings.

Currently, Dick yearns for a long life, in health and comfort, with Mae. Upon asking him the most important lesson he learned throughout his life experiences, he said it was "to treat others the way you want to be treated." I concluded our interview with the question, "A genie appears at your doorstep and tells you that you have three wishes. What would those three wishes be?" Dick's response was good health for those he loves, global peace among individuals, and a reduced rate of poverty in metropolitan areas.

Looking down the road, Dick desires for his kids to remember him and Mae as parents who loved them dearly. Additionally, he hopes that through his own actions, he has instilled in his children the great importance of doing for others as you would do for yourself.

XVI. Jacqueline "Jackie" N.

For Jackie, life as a child was idyllic. Despite being born amid the Great Depression, its impact did not affect her outlook on life. Growing up in Utica, NY, with her parents and older brother Howard, her routine consisted of attending school, engaging in activities, and in her teenage years, working frequently. Sunday afternoons, Jackie and her parents gathered in the car and took a trip to the local farms, where they purchased freshly picked fruits and vegetables which her mother would put in mason jars for the coming winters. In the summertime, she splashed around in the public swimming pool, and during the school year, Jackie was immersed in Girl Scout programs. She attended Hebrew school classes until she was sixteen, when she was confirmed, and continued to sing in the synagogue's choir alongside her mother. Jackie found her escape from the world through reading, a pastime she adopted from her father. Often, Jackie explored the texts her father left around, despite how mature the topics were. Weighty subject matter regarding war and the accompanying devastation were often considered too

155

taboo for children to hear at the time. Jackie's parents strived to shield their children from the blemished aspects of the world, allowing them to enjoy their childhood years. That said, there were a few moments when that facade crumbled, most prominently when Jackie's mother broke down into tears as a result of President Roosevelt's death.

Jackie always cherished playing with her dolls, pretending she was their mother. At the age of eleven, her pastime of doll playing actualized into real responsibility, when Jackie took on the role of babysitter to an eighteen-month-old toddler. Every Saturday, she cared for the young child over a fifteen-hour time frame while the parents were conducting business. For her efforts, she received a total of $3.75 per day. Despite the amount of work involved with taking care of a young child, Jackie was fond of her role, sometimes pretending she was the baby's mother.

Living in a small town, the opportunities for leisure entertainment were minimal. As a teenager, her free time was often spent with her coterie of friends and going out on dates. Because of how popular dancing was for social life, her father instructed both Jackie and Howard on how to dance. Her parents were reasonably lenient and allowed her the independence to safely go on dates with boys. Jackie felt that her parents, especially her mother, held the presumption that her future would be solely as a mother and wife. She resented the fact that her pursuit of a career was not expected, nor encouraged. Expectations for her brother, Howard, were different in this regard.

At the age of fourteen, Jackie obtained official working documentation, permitting her to take on part time hours at various jobs. In high school, one particular position Jackie held was working evenings in the library at Utica's conservative synagogue. One night, while Jackie was sitting in the library, two college students walked in. One of the boys was her husband to be, Karl. Over the years until they eventually got married, Jackie and Karl dated periodically. Visiting his home in Brooklyn, she met his family, and they often celebrated major holidays together.

At the time of Jackie's high school graduation in 1952, U.S. Korean War veterans began to return home and pursue their education. Because of the massive number of veterans who desired to pursue higher education, many universities were operating at full capacity. To deal with this issue, Syracuse University opened up satellite campuses, one of which was placed in Utica, NY. Due to the proximity, both Jackie and her brother attended Syracuse's campus in Utica, making it possible for them to live at home and work while attending classes full-time. Jackie was passionate about her fields of study, English literature and philosophy. Despite earning a merit scholarship that covered a fourth of tuition costs and required her to maintain high grades, Jackie still had to work diligently in three jobs to pay for her studies. In May of 1956, Jackie received her bachelor's degree from Syracuse University.

Directly after she graduated, Jackie enrolled in a six-week training program for teachers supervised by SUNY New Paltz State Teachers College in Farmingdale, NY. At the time, there was a shortage of educators, making the teaching profession attractive as a possible career. Jackie and her fiancé got married in August of 1956, two days after she completed the training program. Jackie moved to Brooklyn where her husband continued his graduate studies. At this time, she became the couple's sole earner and quickly secured a job in Manhattan, transcribing engineers' notes at a division of American Standard. In the spring of 1957, she returned to evening classes at Brooklyn College, where she picked up more graduate-level courses toward a Master of Arts degree.

In June of 1957, less than a year after they had gotten married, Jackie and her husband spontaneously opted to sail to Southhampton, England, and embarked on a nine-week adventure across the European continent. The time was opportune since Karl felt he would never have nine weeks of time off again, and he had been eager to return to visit his place of birth, Vienna. With an itinerary in mind, but no reservations booked whatsoever, they decided the trip's plans would materialize upon their arrival. One of Jackie's fondest memories of the trip occurred in London on their very first night in Europe. She spotted an advertisement for a Shakespearean play featuring Laurence Olivier, Vivien Leigh, and Anthony Quayle. As a lover of literature her entire life, Jackie was ablaze with excitement upon considering the prospect of attending this production. Together, they went to see the play, a memory Jackie forever cherishes. After they explored England, the excitement did not cease, for they then traveled to Denmark, Sweden, Germany, Holland, Belgium, France, Italy, and Austria. With one of Jackie's cousins and his wife, the two couples rendezvoused in a small hotel on the left bank in Paris, costing a mighty seventy-five cents per room per night of stay. The fee not only covered the price of the room, but also coffee and a basket of croissants daily. The trip opened her eyes to a world distinct from what she had known. It was miraculous.

Before leaving for this nine-week European escapade, Jackie decided she would not return to her job in Manhattan since the office was soon relocating to Connecticut and she could not commute from Brooklyn. However, a lack of job security did not prove to be a barrier whatsoever. Only one day after arriving home to Brooklyn, Jackie went into the Brownsville neighborhood and obtained a teaching position within one of the elementary schools in the district. Although she had attended a six-week teaching training course, she had no prior classroom experience. This was yet another new experience Jackie was willing to take on. The following Monday post securing the job, Jackie entered the classroom filled with thirty-eight second graders. She was surprised to learn Spanish was the native language of many of her students and they could not communicate well in English. Without any teaching assistant, as well as the language barrier present, this experience certainly proved challenging. The school was situated within a neighborhood deemed rough, which forced Jackie to find ways to navigate to and from work every day safely. When behavior issues arose among the children, she found it sometimes impossible to connect with the parents for a meeting. Most of the fellow teachers were elderly, yet there was one other young educator with whom Jackie became close friends. Often, the two teachers combined their classes for the music period to collaboratively lead the children. Jackie played the piano and her friend led the singing. Jackie found the students to be adorable and thoroughly enjoyed the experience. In her second year of teaching, Jackie became pregnant with her first child. She had to take precautions with her clothing, often choosing loose garments, for she knew the principal would fire her immediately if her pregnancy was discovered. At the time, the system did not allow pregnant teachers to continue to be employed.

When her first child, David, was born in October of 1959, her full-time role shifted to becoming a mother. In July 1960, the young family relocated to North Carolina, where Karl was stationed at Camp Lejeune working in the Naval Hospital. While living there, Jackie gave birth to her second son, Peter. When Karl's two-year service term was completed, the now four-person family moved back up north to New York City where Karl completed his residency. The next move was to Queens, NY, where Karl opened a private practice and Jackie had her third son, Edward in 1965. In Queens, Jackie became involved with the Parent-Teacher Association and maintained a busy social life. In 1972, the family moved yet again to Long Island.

The couple also took the opportunity to travel as much as possible, both with and without the children. Rather than enrolling the boys in summer camp like many other kids at the time, Jackie and Karl felt as if seeing the world would broaden their sons' perspectives. On multiple occasions during summer breaks, the family spent weeks in Engelberg, Switzerland, where they rented a home that served as their base for exploration. Near their vacation home was Mt. Titlis, a perfect place to ride cable cars to the lofty summit. Sometimes on their assent, they would pass directly through the clouds. Every so often, they would stop midway on the ride, and their boys would run down the mountains through the lush meadows. Switzerland was a peaceful getaway, serving as a strong contrast to their hectic lifestyle in the city. Often, when the boys were young, their summer trip to Europe was supplemented with a two-week stay in a rental cottage on Cape Cod. Beyond that, the family adventured on cruises and through numerous U.S. national parks, where they listened to the wonderful park rangers discuss the various wildlife that inhabited the area.

Upon moving to Long Island in the early seventies, Jackie returned to work on a part-time basis. After an extended hiatus, with her children busy in school every day, Jackie was bored and felt impelled to work. It was something she needed to do for her own wellbeing. As someone who had traveled extensively, she thought mapping out travel experiences for others would be a new and refreshing career change. At the same time, Jackie and her husband were growing in diverging directions. Subsequently, Jackie and Karl divorced.

Jackie ramped up the number of hours worked, so that in time, she became a full-time employee and later the manager at the travel agency. While at the job, she continued to raise her children and travel when she had time. After fourteen years at the initial agency, Jackie switched to a managerial role at a new travel firm. She oversaw the other agents and continued to develop client itineraries. Beyond planning the trip outlines, she booked lodging accommodations that she recommended based on her own travel experiences. At the second agency, Jackie spent the next twenty-one years of her career. Finally, Jackie embarked on her last role before retirement. Here she oversaw one international corporate account. Her work entailed connecting with national clients to coordinate the transport and delivery of their high-end vehicles from Europe to the United States in conjunction with their individual European itineraries.

At the age of eighty-three, Jackie retired from her fulfilling work. Upon doing so, in 2018, she moved to a senior community, although it was not initially her idea to relocate. Her children proposed the idea, as they believed it would be better for her to live in proximity to one of them. She moved to Orchard Cove and became fond of its warmth, friendly ambiance, and sense of community. Jackie ultimately found contentment.

Jackie loved her role as a mother, more than anything else in the world. While she found pleasure in her career and was passionate about her travels, her priority was to be a good mother to her boys and instill ethical values. Having her three children "was the best thing she ever did in life," she said, for they give her "enormous pleasure." About her boys, Jackie said, "I like them. I really do like them." Tragically, Jackie suffered an immeasurable loss when her youngest son, Edward, died at the age of forty-one. Edward's legacy lives on through many avenues, perhaps most prominently through his own son, Alex. In addition to her grandson, Jackie is the proud grandmother of four lovely girls. She considers this a special gift, especially since she had never had daughters of her own. She cherishes the good relations that she shares with her grandchildren and is thankful for their spontaneous calls. They often confide in her for advice because they trust her judgment and willingness to keep information secure. Jackie explained, "I often told my grandkids that the [information] goes in one ear and stops at the top [of the brain]." With her wonderful sons, lovely daughters-in-law, and beautiful grandchildren, Jackie feels unbelievably blessed. As an eighty-five-year-old woman, very little matters to Jackie other than their happiness and wellbeing. She hopes that they always remember her as a decent, fair, and kind individual.

Jackie believes in the importance of family and holding closely onto one's loved ones. She relishes the moments spent with them, especially during holiday times. Passover was and continues to be commemorated with the immediate family and distant relatives, sharing a large seder and meal. Throughout her years, Jackie has also maintained the outlook that kindness to others is essential, and anger takes and absorbs too much energy. In her eyes, nothing positive comes from being angry. It is not a constructive emotion.

As a travel agent and an avid traveler, Jackie has been fortunate enough to visit places worldwide. Often, amid her career, individuals asked her, "What do you get from travel?" Her answer is simple. "There are similarities between all people." Although Jackie has immersed herself into countless cultures, tried a variety of cuisines, and witnessed different religions, through her travels she has also noticed that there is an underlying commonality among people, despite what one's background is. Individuals all vie for the same things in their lifetime, whether that be food, water, peace, comfort, or love. She strongly wishes that everyone shared this lens. In Jackie's view, the congruities that all humans share should unite people together, not divide.

Jackie considered her father to be one of the most influential figures in her lifetime. He exuded intelligence and never failed to demonstrate diligence. His love and acceptance for both of his children were evident. Her father, Edward, exemplified the motto of never giving up, for he did not walk away from challenges in his life merely because he did not like them. As Jackie learned from her father, "With things you cannot change, all you can do is decide how to deal with it. That is the only control you have."

For a portion of her life, Jackie felt as if she was preoccupied with embodying the person that others expected her to be. For a while, she conformed herself to others' standards, believing that was the proper thing to do. However, after some time, Jackie stopped and said to herself, "Where am I?" Determining who she was indeed took a while, but with time, she found herself. At the age of eighty-five, Jackie determined she does not have to be anyone that she does not want to be. Without a doubt, this is an important lesson learned with time.

XVII. Gertrude "Trudy"

In 1939, Trudy and her sister, Lotte, made the challenging, yet necessary, choice to abandon the town they grew up in, Stuttgart, Germany, in exchange for a safer life in England. In addition to their home, the girls' parents remained behind, as they were amid the process of securing proper travel documentation. Rather than meeting their daughters in England, in 1941, her parents left for the United States on one of the last ships from Germany. At the time of her transition to England, Trudy was only twenty years of age, unsure of what the future would resemble. However, she was aware that as a Jewish individual, living in Germany placed her in grave danger. Upon the Nazis coming to power in 1933, life as Trudy knew it changed. In reference to the Nazis' behaviors, her grandmother, Friedericke Hirsch, often said, "That it would soon all pass." Many believed that German citizens would rise against the Nazis and not tolerate the treatment. Yet, as history reveals, it did not soon pass. Many German Jews lost their jobs, including Trudy's father, who was the director of the nation's largest shoe factory. Jewish musicians were forbidden from performing for the general public, which forced them to find other outlets, and Jewish citizens were banned from attending theatres or movies. Some musicians found work through a Jewish organization that hired artists and hosted concerts or plays. Trudy served as an usher for these events, allowing her to view performances free of charge. As the years passed on and the war's initiation neared, the presence of antisemitic perspectives were pervasive throughout Germany. As Trudy said, the Nazis' motto was, "We won't throw them out, but we will make it so they are anxious to leave" in regard to the German Jewish people.

Despite having to leave, Trudy possessed fond memories of her juvenile years living in Stuttgart, describing it as reasonably carefree. When young, she felt pride in her German nationality. During her formative years, Trudy was friends to many, some of whom did not even identify as Jewish. This included her best friend, Irene. Before the arrival of the Nazis, Trudy could not remember a time where she was discriminated against due to her religious heritage. She was brought up Jewish as a child, but her family only celebrated significant holidays such as Passover and Hannukah. Trudy generally spent her Easter school vacation in Ulm, the city where her mother grew up, often attending large seders for Passover with the extended family. In Germany, her family displayed a Christmas tree because they appreciated the aesthetic. That said, the Hannukah menorah was always placed nearby, and the candles were lit nightly. While girls in Germany did not have Bat Mitzvahs when Trudy was thirteen, she was confirmed on the holiday of Shavuot with the other five girls who turned thirteen that same year.

As a teen, Trudy engaged in a Jewish youth organization that had affiliate chapters in each German city. The organization was divided into boy and girl groups, as well as older and younger subparts. Trudy was active within the older girls' section, yet also led a group for younger girls. She attended meetings with other leaders, went on hikes with her fellow members, and met once a week to sing and discuss issues. Because she could not immerse herself in activities teenagers usually lean toward, such as movie watching, Trudy's leisure time was generally spent with her Jewish youth group. Growing up, she also utilized her time with her family. She was the oldest of three girls in her family, but her youngest sister sadly passed away at three years old due to Tay-Sachs disease.

Upon moving to England, where Trudy remained for the war's duration, she became a domestic employee. First, she took on a role as a cook general for a family household. Soon enough, she was hired by two parents in need of a nanny for their disabled child. Here, she stayed for three years. The child's mother, whom Trudy admired very much, was named Peggy. When Trudy had her daughter many years later, she called her Margaret, but

169

nicknamed her Peggy, to honor the mother's memory. Due to the child's condition, a physical therapist would often visit the family's home, engaging in exercises to build strength and increase function. Upon witnessing the physical therapist helping the child, Trudy thought to herself, "I do not want to be a nanny for the remainder of my life." Trudy would often heed the exercises that the child's physical therapist taught, allowing her to learn and thus help the child in the intervening period between therapy sessions.

Physical therapy intrigued her, and she knew that was the career she wanted to pursue. Thankfully, she was able to secure a scholarship to pay for the certification courses. Trudy studied for two and a half years, and at the end of that period, she was a licensed physical therapist. There was reciprocity between the United States and Britain at the time, meaning that she could technically find work as a physical therapist immediately when she eventually moved to America.

After receiving her certificate, Trudy went directly to work as a physical therapist in England. Her first job was at the Association for the Aid of Crippled Children, where she worked for two and a half years. When the war officially ended, Trudy served as a physical therapist at Leeds Hospital in England. Because of her knowledge of German, she found herself helping young German prisoners of war who had been injured.

At the time, her parents resided in the Jamaica neighborhood of Queens, NY. To make ends meet, her mother had taken on a role as a practical nurse, and her father pursued a variety of odd opportunities, such as helping individuals complete immigration documentation. They were anxious for their two daughters to join them in America. After acquiring the proper immigration forms, in 1946, Trudy and her sister moved to the United States to live with their parents in New York City. They traveled by ship, where they both served as stewardesses. The sisters were eager to see their parents, for it had been seven years since they originally left Germany. Upon arriving for the first time in America, Trudy emphasized how strange it felt. The culture contrasted so strongly with what she had been accustomed to while living in England. She termed it as "more aggressive," which took her some time to adjust to. For example, shortly after coming to America, Trudy recalled entering a grocery store asking, "Could I have a loaf of bread and a pound of butter?" The store teller looked at her, confused, responding, "Well, do you have money to purchase the bread?" The shop owner misinterpreted her question, thinking that she was begging for food, but Trudy was merely politely posing the question. Life in the United States, especially in the city, diverged from the social norms in England.

Because of the agreement between England and the United States, Trudy's physical therapy certification was respected when she arrived in America. She quickly secured a role as a physical therapist at the Stuyvesant Polyclinic Hospital in Manhattan, which allowed her to make a living. Even so, Trudy felt it would be best for her career to obtain an American license. While working, she attended New York University (NYU) and received a degree in physical therapy. From that point onwards, she became a full-fledged pediatric physical therapist working in the field until her retirement in 1978. Much of her career was spent in the New York City public school system, providing physical therapy to children with cerebral palsy, muscular dystrophy, cystic fibrosis and other physical challenges.

While living in America, Trudy was introduced by her friends to her future husband, Joe. He, too, immigrated from Germany and was Jewish. Her first encounter with Joe was through a double date, where the two couples went on a hike with one another. Their relationship took time to develop due to Trudy's hesitation. She knew that their backgrounds differed significantly, especially in terms of education, which initially made her skeptical about their relationship's possible future. With that said, in 1952, Trudy and Joe got married. They found that they were perfectly compatible, as they both enjoyed educating themselves by reading and attending concerts and interesting lectures. Trudy stated that her husband Joe was wildly curious and took an interest in various topics. The couple found their home within the Queens borough of New York City. Here, they raised their two sons, Peter and Tom, and their daughter, Margaret, who goes by Peggy among family members. While they did not keep Shabbat, Trudy and Joe raised their children Jewish. The kids were enrolled and attended Hebrew school classes, and the family always went to High Holiday services in September.

After retiring from work, Trudy continued to find ways to help others. She became a volunteer, serving at a nursing home in the Jamaica neighborhood of the city. There, she would stroll around with a well-loaded cart, selling snacks and sweets to the residents. Trudy went to the grocery store and purchased the items, which were then sold to the residents at cost. The highlight of the residents' days was when she made her rounds. When she first began this role, the cart only had a few cookies and candy bars. However, as the residents started asking for new items, Trudy undertook to fulfill their diverse requests. Until she left New York, she interacted with the community and immensely enjoyed doing so. By the end of her visits in 2016, the cart possessed an assortment of twenty-five items—everything from soup to nuts.

Sadly, after a beautiful fifty-one-year marriage, Joe passed away in 2003 from cancer, forcing Trudy to live alone in New York City. In 2016, at the age of ninety-seven, Trudy made the challenging decision to renounce her NYC home and move to

Orchard Cove instead. Her children persuaded her that living by herself was no longer a wise idea. However, before moving, Trudy left on a trip across the nation to visit her sister living in Alaska.

Rather than purchasing and decorating a new home, Trudy and her children concurred that it would be best to find a community to live in, where she could engage in activities and encounter new people. Trudy indeed found her niches within the senior community at large. She frequented many of the community-wide events, series of lectures, and concerts.

With a robust celebration, Trudy commemorated her 100th birthday at Orchard Cove in June of 2019. It was a special day for her. As a centenarian, Trudy is sharper than ever. She is fluent in two languages, German and English, and also knows French and Latin bits. Looking back upon her life, Trudy states that her grandest accomplishment was raising her children to be decent individuals. She is so proud of them, for they are all intelligent, community-minded, and active. She lived her life with the priority to take an interest in and care for other people, a value which she hopes to have instilled within her children. In her eyes, the best aspect of being a parent or a grandma to her three grandkids was watching them grow up and seeing how their perspectives were shaped by the continuously evolving world. If given three wishes, Trudy hopes that her children will remain healthy, she will live many more years in good physical and mental health, and finally, the world will remain peaceful. She hopes to be remembered by her family as an individual who loved them, who was kind to others, and who always placed emphasis on others before herself.

XVIII. Jackie T.

At an age earlier than most, Jackie understood the importance of being there for her loved ones. Both of her parents were German, yet her mother was born in the United States, and Jackie's father had immigrated from Germany to America years before his daughter was born. On the brink of World War II, Jackie's father's family, who identified as Jewish, still resided in Germany. While few could have foreseen the tragedies that would unfold during the war before its beginning, there was undoubtedly an antisemitic sentiment present in Germany, hinting future danger. Thus, in 1938, when Jackie was nine years old, her father helped his immediate family flee to safety by bringing them over to the United States from Germany. All of a sudden, the radius of Jackie's family circle had expanded significantly. For the first time, she met her grandparents, aunts, uncles, and four cousins. Although her family was Jewish, her parents never emphasized Jewish customs or holidays, at least during her young years. However, when her father's family arrived in America, Jackie's parents decided the time was right for her to be exposed to her religion. Thus, she was enrolled in Sunday School and, when she was ten years old, attended her first Passover seder. Later in life, Jackie and her family observed some Jewish traditions, such as holding a seder, but it was purely for familial purposes. Jackie distanced herself from Judaism, as her personal values conflicted with the religious stories and perspectives.

For the first seven years of her life, Jackie lived in the Bronx borough of New York City. She was the oldest out of four children in her family. Her first sister, Rhoda, was born five years after her, her brother Richard was born three years after Rhoda, and finally, Danny was born when Jackie was sixteen years of age. While living in the city, her family occupied a small apartment. It was located across the street from an expansive park where Jackie would often dawdle by roller skating. During her year of kindergarten, Jackie drew a photo of her father on a large vessel, serving as a visual recreation of her father leaving, alongside his older brother, on a massive ship known as the Normandy en route to Europe. For a few months, he visited his family there. Watching her father depart on the boat was a memory that remained prominent in Jackie's mind for years after.

As the family grew in size, Jackie's parents decided to purchase a home in the suburban area of New York City, in an area called

Flushing. There, Jackie attended school, which she adored very much. Living a mile away, she had to walk to school and back every day, despite the weather circumstances. Beyond that, students were required to go home for lunch. Thus, at noon on weekdays, Jackie treaded one mile home, ate lunch, and speedily made her way back. She had to return at five to one, or else she was considered tardy. Sometimes, during her short visit home, her mother would give her a quarter to make a trip to the local convenient store and purchase a loaf of bread to go with lunch. From a young age, she was always involved in assisting her mother, priding herself in being a proper child who abided by her parents' requests. Jackie contrasted sharply with her sister Rhoda, who possessed a feisty personality. She was responsible, mature, efficient, reliable, and always setting her expectations high for herself—characteristics her parents instilled within her. These traits remained with Jackie until adulthood. When her brother, Danny, was born in 1945, Jackie took on the responsibility of caring for her infant brother. Her mother was not well to take care of the baby. At this point, Jackie was a teenager, and her friends thought it was peculiar for her to take care of her brother. Yet, Jackie was not bothered. Her priority was to be there for her loved ones, a value she learned from her father.

Her father, Max, was a self-employed manufacturer of fire escapes. Despite the financial hardship that American families experienced during the Depression era, Max always managed to make a living, even during the grimmest of circumstances. While the family was never in need of necessary supplies, Jackie noted that she was raised very frugally. Being careful with money was ingrained within her. Waste, in her dictionary, was a term unheard of, and she recycled items before it was a popular thing. Because of her careful habits, many have coined her with the name of "minimalist." In suit with this, during her childhood, Jackie would play games on the street that would require absolutely no equipment. Games were born from her imagination, allowing her and her friends to stay occupied for hours upon end. Sometimes, however, a ball or a deck of cards was required to play catch or "May I?" with her peers. These were activities she always relished. When Jackie got older, her time was spent taking long walks with her friends and conversing. As an early teen, before caring for her brother, Jackie spent her summers going to a camp where she created lifelong friendships. One friend, Lolly, whom she met when she was fourteen in Flushing, attended Jackie's ninetieth birthday party in November of 2019.

Jackie met her husband, Dick, when she was seventeen years old. He had just returned from serving in the war, where he specialized in training war pigeons as a member of the U.S. Army. The local temple had begun to promote events for returning soldiers to meet the local young crowd to help them transition into their old lives. Jackie, an attendee of one of these events, met her husband through a ping-pong game. Because of this, at the age of ninety years old, Jackie continues to play ping-pong. The pastime always reminds her of her beloved husband Dick.

After dating for about one year, the couple officialized their love for one another by getting married. At the time, Jackie was eighteen years of age and halfway through her studies to receive an undergraduate degree at Mills College. Upon getting married, she decided to leave school, but she knew she would return to college someday. At this point, she was "ready to make her own nest." Although she was young, Jackie was mature and equipped to run her own home. Overseeing her brother when he was a baby provided her a glimpse of what motherhood would resemble, and she was excited to have children to call her own. Jackie and Dick had three children, two boys named Andy and David, and one girl named Nina. Eventually, in 1959, Jackie received her bachelor's degree from Hofstra University, where she majored in education. Her children were young at the time, thus she was left with no choice but to attend night classes. It would not have been a possible feat without help from her mother, sister, and brother who put the kids to bed when she went to class.

At the age of forty, Jackie became a teacher to elementary school-aged children at a public school in Whitestone, a neighborhood in Queens. Later, she taught within the Garden City School System in Long Island. Because of how much she enjoyed teaching, she stuck with this career until retirement. As a young girl, Jackie never believed she would be anything other than a wife and mother. Thus, she was thrilled to have found a career she could immerse herself in. Second to her role as a mom to her three children, she earned the new educator title. Jackie found teaching came easy to her; it was natural. Her favorite aspect was the spontaneity of the role, for she never knew what the children would do, say, or react to. Beyond that, it was exciting for her to see the children absorb the information outputted to them. Jackie had the unique opportunity to watch the kids learn, and through this process, grow as intellectuals. It was a fulfilling role for her. She continued her teaching career until her early fifties.

In 1983, Jackie and Dick purchased a home in Arizona, the first time she lived anywhere but New York. At this point, Dick had taken an early retirement package, their children were all grown up, and most prominently, the couple felt ready for a change. Beyond that, they believed the warm climate would be ideal for Dick, who had breathing issues. Jackie and Dick had friends who moved to Arizona prior and loved it. It was certainly not a difficult decision.

Upon arriving, Jackie stopped teaching in her own classroom, but she did substitute for a little while. Dick worked as an adjunct professor at Arizona State University, where he taught business classes. He also continued to pursue his unusual passion of raising and racing homing pigeons, a pastime connected to his efforts serving in the war. Jackie discovered quickly that substitute teaching was not the path she wanted to take, yet she did like working with children. So, she began to preoccupy herself in volunteering opportunities. She served as a teacher assistant at the local school, as well as a tour guide for school children at the Phoenix Zoo. At the Scottsdale Contemporary Art Museum, she led museum tours, and she described the paintings to the kids. At the local library, Jackie volunteered to teach adults learning English as their second language.

While living in Arizona allowed Jackie and her husband to conduct a comfortable lifestyle, the one drawback was their children and grandchildren lived a distance away. When her four grandchildren were born, Jackie was there to help out. However, as they grew up, Jackie and her husband stayed connected to their lives through phone calls. In the wintertime, the children and grandchildren would often take trips to Arizona, and conversely, in the summertime, Jackie and Dick went to visit them.

Jackie emphasized how wonderful it was to see her grandchildren, who were once babies, grow into successful young adults. Beyond that, she has cherished seeing her own children take on the challenges and triumphs of parenthood, and in Jackie's words, "start, develop, and grow their own nests."

Traveling was one of Jackie's most treasured things to do. Prior to living in Arizona, Dick and Jackie purchased a motor home and went on numerous vacations cross country. Once, they embarked on a six-week road trip spanning the United States and beyond, traveling from New York to Texas to Canada. They also extended their horizons by visiting Puerto Rico, Israel, Hawaii, Canada, and numerous countries in Europe, including Spain, Germany, and Belgium. When living in Arizona, Jackie and Dick became connected to International Executive Service Corps (IESC), and through this program, went to Kazakhstan and Uzbekistan. Here, Jackie engulfed herself in the community and interacted with the local citizens, while her husband worked on a project to enable citizens the opportunity to engage in business. Beyond that, they went to Ukraine and Russia, where Dick spent his time modernizing an ice cream factory to increase operational efficiency. When asked what her favorite place was, she said it was an impossible choice. It depended on what she was traveling for, whether it be relaxation, adventure, or to see a loved one. All the places she ventured to had positive characteristics about them.

Regretfully, Jackie's dear husband of sixty years, Dick, passed away in 2008 while they lived in Arizona. Jackie continued to stay in their home for eight more years, whereupon she decided that it was time to move closer to one of her children. Although she had excellent health, she felt it was the most sensible decision to find a new place to live. Thus, in 2016, Jackie moved to Orchard Cove to live in proximity to her daughter, Nina. She quickly involved herself in an array of activities. As a social individual her entire life, she became a buddy on the hospitality committee, engaged in bridge games with experienced players, knitted hats and scarves to donate to orphanages and shelters, and was fond of conversations with her fellow neighbors. When the coronavirus pandemic changed life as it once was, Jackie maintained a positive outlook, viewing it as a test to her resilience. She stated, "People are like tea bags; you never know how strong you are until you are put in hot water."

Family was always something that Jackie cherished immensely. She always had looked forward to special occasions, holidays, and get-togethers. She was grateful for her family's healthy relations and the sense of humor prevailing among her loved ones. Beyond that, Jackie appreciated how her family was so open and warm. At the age of ninety, she is a proud mother, grandmother, and great grandma to six. It is Jackie's hope to always be remembered by her overall good spirit, practical approach to life, sensibility, and without a doubt, her sharp wit.

Acknowledgements

When I began The Legacy Project, never in my wildest dreams did I think the journey would conclude with a published book. Yet, here we are.

However, none of this would have been possible without a number of people who have cheered me on, supported me, and provided insight as I ventured through this book-writing journey. I am grateful for all who are named below, as well as the countless others who have shaped me in ways both small and large.

Jennifer Mazzola, for being one of my high school best friends and the best co-worker, as well for being so enthusiastic and supportive from day one of this project. From attending a number of the interviews with me, typing up interview notes, and always being willing to listen to my sometimes (admittedly) wild ideas without judgment, I have so much gratitude. A grand thank you to you, Jenny.

ACKNOWLEDGEMENTS

Ilana Klarman, for believing in my vision and working with me to get the project off the ground. You were the first individual who I came into contact with to discuss the idea, and it was because of your dedication to the project that it gained so much success from the get-go.

Susan Tovsky & Jacqui Mutascio, for all of your help determining the logistical aspects of this project, meeting with me to discuss further project developments, answering the countless number of emails that I sent, and leading me to solutions when the COVID-19 pandemic complicated the process.

Bernard Mendillo, for bestowing your many years of book-writing expertise and sharing your insight on the publishing process. I am grateful to have met you at my first Canton Writes Competition when I was in elementary school, and I am glad to have reconnected many years later. As a first-time author, I was entering the book publishing process blind, and I am infinitely grateful for the direction you provided.

Ashley Brown, for being such a fantastic editor to work with and so flexible in deadlines when I needed just "a few more days." Thank you for reviewing the book with such precision and care and for being so prompt in your delivery. I look forward to working with you again when I publish a second book someday.

Rachel Kessler, for being not only an incredible person in my life but also the world's best cheerleader. Thank you for your support throughout the process, fresh perspectives, and numerous offers to help. I am so appreciative to have a friend like you.

To all my past teachers, and in particular Rebecca Hahn and Edward Amico, for having such an immense impact on me during my high school experience, inspiring me to dream bigger, supporting me in the craziest of my endeavors, sparking my interest in community service, refining my writing abilities, and being so invested in my success.

To Grandma Loie, Grandma Phyllis, Ikey, Jan Jan, Scott, Min, Qiana, Brad, Kim, and Elyse for being the best grandmothers, aunts, uncles, and cousins a girl could dream of having. Thank you for being my support system. I love you all a trillion times over.

All my friends, both new and old, for supporting me and listening to me ramble about this book non-stop. Thank you for letting me talk your ears off. I love you guys.

Lexi, my cute miniature schnauzer, for being my snuggle buddy and one heck of a listener. I am grateful for all the joy you bring into my life.

ACKNOWLEDGEMENTS

Mom and Dad, for everything and more. Thank you for not only pushing me to reach my potential but encouraging me to pursue new feats, despite how ridiculous they may seem. You guys are my backbone, and it was because of you both that I decided to chase after this idea from the start. I am grateful for the many, many, many hours you spent generating ideas with me, helping me navigate the book publishing process, serving as my unofficial editors, and working with me to make this book materialize. I love you both so, so, so, much. Words cannot encapsulate how grateful I am for the both of you.

All the residents from Orchard Cove Senior Living Community who were interviewed, for your willingness to partake in this journey with me. Thank you for welcoming me into your homes with such open arms, telling your stories with such candidness, sharing your cherished photos, and developing friendships with me. I am incredibly grateful for your unwavering patience and the number of hours each of you spent, both for the interview and during the revision process, to ensure a quality product. I have gained valuable life lessons through our conversations, all of which will guide me in the future.

I am so deeply saddened by the fact that a few of the interviewees, whose stories are presented in the book, have passed away since the writing process began. While they will be deeply missed, I appreciate the moments I spent with each of them and am honored to have heard their stories. This book pays tribute to the memories of these individuals, whose stories are, hopefully, now preserved for years to come.

A Trip Down Memory Lane

In the following pages, you will find a collection of images graciously provided to me by the individuals featured in this book. The images depict a wide array of life phases—from childhood, to adolescence, to adulthood, and finally, photographs taken in recent years. It is my hope that these pictures enrich the reading experience, by putting a face to the name of the individuals that you have learned so much about. I have also included some quotes that have been gathered from the interviews.

Faye, as a Cadet Nurse
1944

Carolyn "Hooky",
as a toddler

Fran, on a pony
1938

Zecil

Geri, five years old

Gertrude "Trudy",
eighteen years old

Ina, adolescent years

Bud, three years old

Neil, age seventeen

194

Diana

Arielle & Joan
2019

Richard & his wife, Mae

Irene & her great-
Granddaughter, Aliyah

Jacqueline "Jackie" N.

Fran & her husband,
in Thailand

Shelagh

Ina, at Western Wall
in Jerusalem

Jackie T.

Bud & Roz

Geri,
Graduating from BU
Master's Program

Trudy, her sister Lotte, & her Father Theo,
Vacationing on Island of Sylt 1932

Fran & her soon-to-be
husband,
Senior Prom

Richard "Dick"

Neil, on a sailboat

Jacqueline "Jackie" N.

Geri, with her children & grandchildren

Irene

Iris

If you had the power to solve one problem in the world, what would it be?
"That's easy. Everyone will say the same thing—world peace among individuals. It is impossible to create total peace, for every individual is fighting their own demons."
-Iris

Zecil

Roz, comparison through the years

Ina, as a young girl

Joan

Richard & his wife, Mae
on their engagement

Faye

"I gave a lot to my community, but at the expense of my own family.
I believe my own kids are givers now in their own right because of the role model I was to them.
One of my children once said,
'I am a giver because of you mom.' "
-Carolyn "Hooky"

Carolyn "Hooky"

Ina, on her wedding day

Richard with his three sons:
Gary, Brad, & Glenn

Fran

Shelagh

Geri (right) and her sister, Selma (left)

"I was high on life.
I don't think I ever came down."
-Charles "Bud"

Roz & Bud with
three daughters Barbara, Lisa, & Sherri

Iris

"Nowadays, there is a lack of family values. The fact
that both mothers and fathers need to work, in a
financial sense, is awful because children should have
a parent there for comfort and support. Family life
used to have more substance. Without technology,
daily life was more vibrant, and young adults could
communicate feelings with emotion."
-Zecil

Zecil

Gertrude "Trudy" & husband Joe,
Norway 1975

Richard, his wife Mae, and three sons

Jackie. T (bottom right)
& family

Neil with his daughters Phyllis &
Vicki, two sons-in-law, and four
grandchildren

Trudy & her children at 1964 World Fair

Neil & his wife, Sandie

Interview Questions

Below are the original questions created for The Legacy Project interviews. The questions are broken up into four categories. While these questions are not all-encompassing, and while the interviews often strayed away from the questions listed, they certainly helped to spark conversation. I have included them here with the hope that you, the readers, may find them useful to initiate your own discussion with a loved one.

Heritage and Values

1. Where were you born? What, if any, connections do you have to your place of birth?

2. How do you feel as if your family's nationality has shaped who you are today?

3. If you were not born in the United States, what can you recall about your experience traveling to America? What possessions did you take? How do you remember this process? What did it feel like to enter America? What expectations did you have about the country? Where did your family first settle and why?

4. How did your family celebrate important holidays when you were younger? What were your favorite holidays? Did your family have any specific traditions?

5. What do you know about your family name? What does it signify to you? To your knowledge, has this name remained the same throughout time?

6. What languages do you speak? Where did you learn these languages? Why is learning multiple languages important?

7. What family traditions are important to you?

8. What does your heritage mean to you? Did religion play a large factor in your life? If so, in what ways?

Childhood, Teenage Years, and Marriage

9. What was life like when you were a child? What was your favorite toy? What did you do for entertainment? Did you have siblings? What was your neighborhood like?

10. Did your parents both work? What did they do for a living?

11. What do you recall as your favorite childhood memory?

12. What was responsibilities did you have as a teenager? Were there any expectations regarding the way you should act?

13. What did you do for fun as a teenager? Did you go to high school prom? Were there any phrases or terms that were popular when you were a teen?

14. Did you become a Bar/Bat Mitzvah? If yes, what did this mean to you?

15. Did you go to college? If so, which one and what did you study?

16. Were you ever married? If so, how did you meet your spouse? What age were you when you got married?

17. What was the hardest decision you made while raising your family?

18. What is the best thing about being a parent or a grandparent?

Living through Prominent Times in History

19. Did your family ever serve in the military? Where were they stationed?

20. How did war impact your life, if at all? What can you remember about society's outlook on war at the time? What were your personal sentiments towards war?

21. Do you remember the beginning of WWII? D-Day? What do you remember about the end of the war?

22. Who you believe was the most influential president in your lifetime? What did they do that sticks out to you?

23. Do you recall any fads (i.e. clothing, hairstyles, cars) when you were younger? In what time period(s) were these popular?

24. What is the most astonishing technology change that you have seen in your life? (i.e. color television, electric fridge, fax machine, cordless phone, the Internet)

25. What do you remember about the first man walking on the moon (1969)?

26. What major events in history had the greatest impact on your life? (i.e. Great Depression, Attack on Pearl Harbor)

Learned Lessons through Experience

27. What did you do for a living? Did you find fulfillment?

28. What are the major values you lived your life by?

29. What is most important to your life right now? Why, and how has this changed throughout your life?

30. Where is the best place you have traveled to? What made this trip so unforgettable?

31. What is the most important lesson you learned in your life? What experience/person taught you this lesson?

32. Who has influenced your life the most?

33. What has been your greatest accomplishment in life? How do you feel this achievement has impacted this world for the better?

34. Do you regret not doing something that you wish you did?

35. What is the biggest challenge you had to overcome in your life? How did you overcome this obstacle, and how do you feel it shaped you into the person you are today?

36. A genie appears at your doorstep and tells you that you have three wishes. What would those three wishes be?

37. If you had the power to solve one issue in the world, what would it be?

38. What would you like your children or grandchildren to remember about you?

39. What do you see when you look at yourself in the mirror?

About the Author

ARIELLE GALINSKY attends Tufts University, where she studies biopsychology, public health, and political science with the hope to find the crossroads between her three academic interests. Within her first semester of college, Arielle immersed herself into the Tufts community by becoming an elected member of the school senate, Speaker Coach for TEDxTufts, writer for the Tufts Daily, and board member for Tufts Best Buddies, NeuroNetwork, and Public Health Society.

Her enthusiasm for writing developed during her formative years, driving her to pursue this passion and win a number of prose and poetry awards in a town wide writing competition. Beyond that, her Jewish values and her belief in *tikkun olam*, or helping others to repair the world, sparked her deep-rooted desire to give back to the community. In the past, she served as a watersport instructor for individuals facing disabilities, aided weekly Special Olympics sports practices, and engaged in a summer-long service internship when the COVID-19 pandemic struck.

If you want to contact Arielle, please email her at
ariellegalinsky@gmail.com or connect with her through LinkedIn!

Printed in Great Britain
by Amazon

56278507R00130